WINLATON

I0429764

The story
of 'a noxious weed'

BOOK THREE

from

The Little Mongrel – free to a ~~good~~ home

by

Merlene Fawdry

Other books by this author

The Hidden Risks– A story of concealment and loss of a family name - ISBN 0-9802845-0-3
The Little Mongrel – free to a ~~good~~ home - ISBN: 978-0-9802845-2-2
In Empty Spaces ISBN 978-0-9802845-2-2
Discourse with Walls ISBN 978-0-9802845-3-9
Seth ISBN 978-1492191506

All place names, events and dates used in this book are factual as remembered by the writer or as provided by other sources, however, some personal names have been changed to protect the rights of the individual.

Web: http://merlenefawdry.blogspot.com.au/
Email: mfawdry@bigpond.net.au

Winlaton – the story of a noxious weed
ISBN-13:978-1500411060
ISBN-10:150041106X

A Noxious Weed

Noxious adj. harmful, unwholesome

Weed n. a wild plant growing where it is not wanted

Contents

Introduction

In the early 1980s, I was employed as a Youth Officer at Western Youth Welfare Service in Melbourne's inner west. This was in the days before de-institutionalisation and the young people we engaged with were among those most psychologically and emotionally damaged, and most frequently discarded, within the state welfare system. With no enforceable rights, they were moved in and around the various institutions, leading to cross-fertilization of deviancy and extreme acting out behaviour. Within the youth work sector a hierarchy had developed where a worker's esteem was self-determined by the level of difficulty posed by the target group they worked with. This began to change in 1982 when the eleven to fourteen-year-olds were targeted for attention within the youth welfare service, referred to collectively as Early Adolescents or, amongst seasoned and often jaded youth officers, the ankle biters.

This move from away from the traditional target group challenged many workers, who needed the continued stroking of their egos provided by the adrenalin rush of working within the unpredictable culture of the 'too hard basket'. Most were reluctant to work with the younger age group, fearing this would damage their professional reputation, so the call went out for expressions of interest from the willing. Seeing this as an opportunity to work proactively toward prevention and deflection from institutional care, working in partnership with the young person, family, and community, I put up my hand.

Engaging with juveniles at this level was both challenging and rewarding, requiring a broad range of skills and innovative responses to maintain home and community placements. Added to this was the segregation from our peers, and occasional derision for working with what they perceived was the softer end of the market.

And so it was that Maurice, my wonderful colleague, and I sat late one afternoon close to mental exhaustion after a day spent chasing

1

truants, dodging emotional fists, interpreting expletives, placating parents and generally calming troubles waters, as we discussed strategies for the following day. My enthusiasm was just slightly higher than Maurice's and he responded to my optimistic babble with, 'Merlene, you're like a noxious weed, you just can't be kept down.'

I thought back to the pesticides used during my youth and their ineffectiveness that, instead of destroying me, nurtured resilience and determination, and I gave thanks for this most wonderful compliment and the other noxious weeds I met along the way.

The back story

I was adopted as a baby into a Tasmanian family to be their fourth child, all adoptees. Their intentions were admirable, their understanding of the needs of adopted children less so, which led to failed relationships and family dysfunction. Being adopted has been the single most damaging event in my life. It robbed me of the knowledge of who I am, leaving me to live in a limbo of disconnectedness, passed into the care of others as a flawed and failed human being. At fourteen, I was sent across the strait to live in Regent House in Elsternwick, Melbourne, a hostel for girls run by the Presbyterian Church. At fifteen I was admitted to Mt St Canice, Convent of the Good Shepherd, at Sandy Bay, Hobart. On discovering I was pregnant, and fearful of detection and having the baby taken from me, I absconded. This is where this part of the story begins.

Home and Away Again

It was strange how, the whole time I'd been in the convent, I just wanted to go home. But I didn't really know if home was the town I grew up in, my family home, or if it was no more than an abstract concept of what I wanted a home to be. Back in Launceston, I was still an absconder from the convent, moving from house to house each night to avoid apprehension. I'd been experiencing heavy cramping ever since I fell from the dormitory window and on the fourth day of freedom I began to bleed heavily. This brought forth doubts as to whether I'd been pregnant after all. I thought perhaps the trauma of convent life had caused my periods to stop and now it had returned with a vengeance. My fellow-absconder, Gaylene, and I sat in the Princes Square and pondered our fate, until my pain became so intense I could no longer sit erect. She was concerned I'd attract attention as I struggled through each pain, and she half carried, half dragged me to a dilapidated toilet block in St John's churchyard.

She'd decided I was having a miscarriage and advised me to let nature take its course, but to do it quietly to avoid investigation and subsequent detection. I curled in foetal position on the concrete floor as the pain rolled over me in waves. The acrid smell of stale urine told of decades of poor aim and the careless attitude of the pious. The filth of the place added another dimension to my degradation. I had only a few seconds respite between the pulsing dragging torture as my baby sought escape from my body, much too early to have any chance of survival. I mourned in emotional and physical agony and I felt the loss of my child long before it had been expelled from my womb. It was my fault. I'd killed my own baby by escaping from the convent. This was to be a greater punishment than any inflicted on me before or after.

The following days passed in a blur of silent grief and the residual pain from an incomplete miscarriage. I felt I should seek medical attention, while other times I thought I hadn't lost the baby after all,

4

that I could feel it in my womb. Gaylene was against seeing a doctor, fearing this would bring about detection for us both, but I was eager to move out of this limbo of hidden existence, and her situation was different from mine. I hadn't been placed in the convent for any legal charge, where she'd been sent to the convent on sentence from the court and, as such, was an escapee. I wanted to negotiate a legal non-return to the convent for myself, but Gaylene saw this as abandonment of her and a disloyalty after she'd helped me through my recent problem.

I met my sister, Marcia, in the street one day and she acted mediator with my parents to broker my return home. I don't know what argument she used, but it was agreed I could live with the family once again. She also had a message from the Launceston police. All I had to do was turn myself in and I wouldn't have to return to the convent. I was tired of running, weary from the miscarriage, and exhausted by the indeterminate state of homelessness.

My decision to give myself up created conflict with Gaylene, but I had an opportunity to return home, while she was always going to have to serve out her sentence. She followed me as close to the police station as she dared, alternating between begging and threatening, with large doses of emotional blackmail, but the thought of legal freedom gave me the courage to defy her and continue on to the police station.

Changing my status with the police was a mere formality. I told them who I was and they filled in some paperwork and told me I was free to go. It was that easy. It didn't make sense to me that I'd had to run away from the convent in order to be released legally. My brother, Bill, went down to Hobart to pick up my belongings the following week and Mother Anselm informed him there'd never been any need for me to run away, if only I'd told her I wanted to leave they would have let me go. I was confused and wondered why I'd been taken back the first time I'd ran away, and then been punished for it. If they'd let me leave by the door I wouldn't have gone out the window, and I wouldn't have lost my baby. I couldn't allow myself the luxury of thinking about it, though.

Once home, I needed to find work, and to find it quickly, if I hoped to remain there. My mother had always made it clear to all of us that a condition of staying in her home was the payment of board, a financial responsibility to be met above all other expenses. I placed my grief at the back of my mind, in the secret place reserved for all of my sorrows, and got on with the job of survival.

I'd heard the factories were beginning to put workers on again and I returned to work at Tamar Knitting Mills, where I'd begun my working life just two years before. I was promoted from pulling ribs to operating an over-locking machine, working in tandem with another operator. I gave no thought as to whether I enjoyed the work or not. I turned up in the morning, did what was required of me, and went home again at night. I made small talk with the other operators, but I was close to nobody. I knew there was no one I could relate to, or who could ever understand my experiences of the past two years. Girls who'd been in homes were looked down on and shunned by the more respectable.

I'd broken up with Phil, the father of my baby, although he wouldn't accept the relationship was over. He turned up everywhere I went. On one occasion, I was walking up Brisbane Street with Marcia and he drove at walking pace alongside of us, tears streaming down his face. I felt a remote sympathy for his emotional pain, but that was all, and I knew this was not enough to base a relationship on. He was a link to the past that had no place in the future, a reminder of what I'd lost. I asked him repeatedly to leave me alone, but he persisted. Marcia felt sorry for him.

'He loves you...don't be such a bitch.'

'I'm not being a bitch. I just don't want to be with him. I don't want to be with anyone.'

He realized he had her compassion, making her a potential ally, so he continued with his pleas. People watched in curiosity as the drama unfolded. It was embarrassing.

'You'll have to do something,' Marcia said, 'people are looking at us. Just get in the car with him.'

'I just can't.'

'I'll come with you then.'

I eventually accepted he had no intention of leaving me alone, so I got in the car with Marcia and asked to be driven home. We sat in the car outside my house for over an hour. He cried and begged, but I remained resolute our relationship had no future. It had caused me a lot of pain and heartache, and a loss so deep I feared the void would never be breached.

I closed my heart to his grief and I left him.

It was no real surprise when, a few days later, I arrived home to find him in conference with my mother in the front lounge. I didn't know which of them arranged the meeting; it was of no consequence to me. She called me into the room, where he stood in teary discomfort.

'I've been talking to Phil,' she said, 'and he wants to marry you.'

I was furious with the underhandedness of it all.

'Well, I don't want to marry him.'

They looked at each other in shock. Had she really thought I'd marry him? He was well aware of my mother's controlling ways. Did he actually believe all he had to do was speak with her and she would force me to marry him? I could see a slow anger rise on my mother's face. This wasn't going as smoothly as she'd intended.

'Well, are you going to get married or what?'

I felt trapped.

I gave my answer as I walked towards the door.

'Or what!'

I could feel the gates of the next institution closing around me. Marriage! And that would be for the rest of my life. I knew I'd have to be extra careful from now on.

Marcia had a disruption to her nursing career and moved back home. On her eighteenth birthday she left the house after everyone else was asleep and never went back. She moved into a flat with Etta, our Gospel Hall friend, and now worked at Patons and Baldwins knitting mill. She was now a common girl like me.

I'd been out of circulation for so long, I felt I didn't know anyone anymore. My relationship with Marcia had improved with the change of address and my only social interaction was with her and Etta. They'd both lost touch with old friends to some degree while living in as student nurses and had befriended outside their own previously known social group. Etta was going out with a worker from the sideshows, seasonal workers who camped at the bottom of Royal Park for the annual Regatta and Henley on Tamar. She introduced Marcia and me to some fighters from Harry Paulsen's boxing troupe, and I started going out with Alfie, a young Aboriginal boy from Mooroopna in Victoria. I'd been brought up to believe carnival workers of a class so low they were to be avoided at all costs so I thought their position to be similar to my own. As an adopted child, in a family of adopted children, many considered us to be undesirable, separated from decent society by virtue of the circumstances of our birth and the bad blood many perceived ran through our veins.

Within this small group of much maligned indigenous people I felt I'd finally found a place of belonging. I admired the way they maintained their dignity, ignoring the superior glances from passers-by, from white-skinned people like me. I tried to practice the same detachment from the opinions of others, but I never quite got it. What they were able to display as quiet self-possession, turned into an air of defiance when I tried it. I was never able to remove myself totally from the opinions of others. I did, however, become quite skilled in avoiding my mother and her matchmaking tendencies. I left for work early in the morning, before her second cup of tea had unglued her eyes and released her acid tongue, and I returned at night after she'd gone to bed. Occasionally our paths crossed and she'd screech at me to get married, or otherwise disappear from her life, but I remained mute to these polite requests.

I practiced maintaining my dignity.

She heard I was keeping company with an Aboriginal boy and waited for me outside work one afternoon, asking me to sit in her car while she spoke to me, one of the few times she'd spoken to me in a rational manner in years. She was concerned I might get pregnant and have a mixed race child. Her worry wasn't racially motivated though, and I understood her apprehension was more about what life would be like for the child. I told her I'd think about what she said, although she didn't need to concern herself about it. I had no intention of having a baby and, even if I did, I could only see the life I imagined I would give a child. My maternal instincts were firmly locked behind the rose coloured glasses of my adolescence. I didn't tell her Alfie would soon be returning to Victoria, nor that I still believed my first boyfriend, Michael, and I would somehow miraculously find each other, get married, and live happily ever after.

Then Marcia came to me with a proposition.

She had a friend who wanted to move to Victoria, but wanted to go with someone who knew their way around Melbourne and Marcia had nominated me. I was hesitant to go. I had my job. It wasn't the greatest, but it was honest work. Home was still a torment, but I'd learnt how to stay out of Mum's way most of the time, and I was still trying to find myself after my convent experience. Marcia was persuasive and I gave in easily enough, especially after she'd already told her friend I would go and my fare had been paid for. She thought it was as much as I could do considering all she'd done for me to aid my return home after the convent. I thought about seeing Alfie after he went back to Victoria and followed the plans of others. It was easier that way.

The day of my departure brought its own anxieties. I had to get my suitcase out of the house without anyone seeing it, in time for my late Sunday afternoon flight, the worst day of the week to avoid people in our house. Everyone was at home on Sundays. As it turned out, my parents, for the first time in my memory, decided to take an after-lunch walk. The little kids had gone on a church outing and everybody else was out.

I couldn't believe my luck.

As soon as my parents disappeared around the bend in the road, I grabbed the old brown suitcase and packed it hastily. With the brown leather strap holding it all together, I left the house, hauling it up the drive and dragging it down the long winding track through the bush to the road below. This was the danger zone, as I didn't know which direction my parents would be walking. Luck was on my side and I made it to the phone box, calling a taxi to take me to the TAA terminal in town.

I had a long time to wait until the coach left for the airport. I found the whole process quite unnerving and expected to feel a tap on my shoulder at any minute. I left my case at the depot and wandered down to Chung Gon's greengrocery, where I bought some grapes, but even the taste of this rare delicacy didn't take the edge off my anxiety. Several times, I made up my mind to just return home, but I knew my absence would already have been noticed and I was afraid of the consequences. I was relieved to finally board the plane and settle back in my seat, my eyes glued to the no smoking light as I waited for it to turn off.

There was no excitement attached to my arrival in Melbourne, only the now familiar sense of disorientation that came with every move. I didn't really know the girl I was to share with. I'd only met her once when Marcia had introduced us. She greeted me at Essendon airport as arranged, with three boys in tow, and they took me to a house in St Kilda. This was a single room, with one double and two single beds, and a kitchen and a bathroom shared with the tenants in two other flats. I realized my presence wasn't needed after all, as she'd already begun a relationship with one of the boys, and was quite happy to be a kept woman.

I called out to see my former employers, Mr and Mrs Baker, and they offered me a job working with them again. I could now work towards getting my own place. I didn't like the close communal living, where beds were used on a rotation basis, and I didn't like living on the edge of the red light district. I couldn't even walk up the street without being accosted by gutter crawlers; men on the lookout for prostitutes or willing sex partners.

Trudy, my old friend from Regent House, was still working at the Caulfield factory, and we teamed up and got our own place. It was a relief only having to share with one other person and not be kept awake each night by sound effects of rampant sex. Trudy wasn't promiscuous so I was happy to settle into domestic harmony with her. We didn't have a lot of money left over once we'd paid the rent and could only afford one hot meal a week, sausages, eggs, and tomatoes with a side serve of chips. It filled my shrinking belly. The rest of the week we scraped by with bread and whatever we could scrounge. We walked the long kilometres to work once we ran out of money for fares, and trekked back home each night, but it was a secure existence. It was strange how, now I had unlimited freedom, there was very little I wanted to do.

I drank sometimes, and sometimes I drank too much, always the cheap sherry that burned in my gut and threatened to return with each greasy mouthful. I could get drunk on a budget and it dulled my pain and made the world look brighter for a while. Trudy and I went out together occasionally, but we had separate lives and individual friends as well. I often caught up with old friends from Regent House, but I didn't begin any new relationships. Then Trudy began to get serious about a boy she'd been seeing and, before I knew it, he'd moved in with us. Our room was too small for the three of us so I looked around for another place closer to work, a home of my own where I wouldn't have to worry about the instability of house mates. I thought if I could save money by not having to pay tram fares then life would be more comfortable, so I looked for somewhere closer to work.

Marcia and Etta arrived in Melbourne en route to Sydney. They stayed with me and other expatriate Tasmanians for a while and eventually moved into a squat in an old mansion in Acland Street. It was supposed to be a rooming house, but it had such easy access through the many casement windows opening off the verandah, no one bothered paying rent. Alfie also arrived in Melbourne and went to stay with his extended family in Fitzroy. He invited me to his cousin's wedding, which was to take place the day after I moved into my new accommodation in a rooming house in Caulfield. Excited to find a place so close to work, I paid my rent in advance and moved my things in the following morning. When I arrived home after work, however, I found my belongings packed and my suitcase, and the owner, waiting for me. He told me it was a men's rooming house and no place for a young girl. The room had been let to me by another tenant by mistake. He gave me back my money.

I was homeless once again. I got a taxi back to St Kilda and went to the Acland Street squat. It wasn't where I wanted to be, but it was a roof over my head until I worked out other accommodation for myself after the weekend. Too late, I realised the cab driver had stolen my purse while pretending to help me out of the car with my suitcase.

Alfie called for me and took me to the wedding. Casual dress, he'd said, but had I known how significant the clothes I wore would become in the weeks ahead, I would have chosen more carefully. As it was, I dressed in keeping with the informal theme of the occasion; pink slacks and shirt and a beige cable knit cardigan. I wore the gold court shoes I was so proud of. Bridget Bardot wore gold court shoes.

The wedding service had been held earlier in the day and by the time we arrived at the old terrace house in Gore Street Fitzroy, the entire wedding party and the guests were in varying stages of intoxication. A brawl had erupted some time before and the groom was in the Fitzroy lockup. His mother had gone down to bail him out and been arrested for being drunk and disorderly. This was to be the fate of anyone seeking to intervene, or negotiate bail, until over half the wedding party had been arrested. I sat in an upstairs bedroom and chatted to the women who lived in the rooming house; one room to each family group. My own life was such a mess I wasn't about to judge how other people lived.

Alfie joined his family and friends in getting drunk and I didn't see much of him throughout the evening. I'd wanted to go back to the squat, preferring that to the unfamiliarity of my surroundings, but I was unfamiliar with the Fitzroy area and there was nobody sober enough to guide me to the tram stop. By the time I'd made myself understood it was too late. I'd missed the last tram for the night. I was somewhere in the middle of Fitzroy, in a house full of inebriated Aboriginals, and I had no way of getting out of there. Someone took pity on me and said I could sleep in a spare single bed on the covered in balcony. I was tired and, although uncertain of my surroundings and the people around me, I accepted the offer gratefully.

I slept fitfully throughout the night. The activity within the house continued unabated. It was not overly loud, just very busy, with doors opening and shutting and people coming and going. Occasionally a voice would be raised in a curse or a laugh, someone would shush the offender and I'd sleep again.

Morning came in a rush of confusion and a clatter of anguish. A lone voice called out a warning, taken up by others and passed along in a chain of alarm.

'Police. The cops are 'ere!'

'Cops! The cops are 'ere.'

'Cops. It's a raid.'

Alfie rushed into the balcony bedroom, 'The cops are 'ere. Get under the bed quick.'

The sound of hurrying feet echoed on the bare wooden stairs, a human stampede born of panic. I sat on the edge of the bed, bewildered by the events unfolding. I made no effort to hide, because I didn't think it had anything to do with me, and Alfie was still exhorting me to get out of sight when the police burst into the tiny space.

'A white girl! There's a white girl in here.'

Faces above blue uniforms peered at me, amazed at my presence. They asked for my name and I answered politely.

'What are you doing here?'

'I came to a wedding and I missed the last tram back home.'

Whatever they'd been looking for, the purpose of the raid appeared to have been forgotten.

'Are you working here?'

'No, I work in Caulfield.'

They talked between themselves, looking at me from time to time. The policewoman, who appeared to be in charge, an older woman in her forties, spoke to me.

'We'll have to take you in.'

'What for? I haven't done anything wrong.'

'Don't pretend you don't know what you're doing here - a white girl in an Aboriginal brothel.'

I didn't understand how I could be in a brothel. All I'd done was go to a wedding. Suddenly the sounds I'd heard during the night made sense to me.

I was the only arrest the police made in that house at Gore Street the morning they raided the Aboriginal brothel. I was ushered down the stairs, past the sad eyes of the occupants, both permanent and temporary, all of us refugees from another time and place. The air was thick with the fumes of stale beer and sherry and cigarettes and the joyous couplings of the previous night had left no sign of lasting happiness. In the clear light of day the displacement and poverty of the urban Aboriginals was obvious and shameful, and I was led away from it into the police car parked at the kerb.

I went passively. I made no resistance, nor did I offer any verbal protest after I left the balcony room. It was a surreal nightmare I'd awaken from soon. But I didn't wake from it, not for the longest time. It became a living nightmare that would gather momentum as the days passed, casting me adrift in the mire of a punitive state welfare system. The cause of the raid on the house had been forgotten with my discovery and I was driven to Russell Street Police Headquarters to be interrogated by a number of different police officers over a period of several hours. I told them everything they wanted to know about me, about my job and my temporary housing setback. I told them nothing about the Gore Street house, because that was all I knew about it, nothing. I told them how old I was.

I was sixteen.

Sixteen and old enough to live on my own if I could show I was able look after myself, and I could have, if I'd just been given the chance.

Eventually I was taken to the office of the arresting officer while she made some phone calls to verify the information I'd given her. She spoke with my employer, who offered to accommodate me until he found me somewhere decent to live, and then to supervise my living arrangements. He was willing to have me signed into his care, but it was too late, as the policewoman explained to me.

'I wish I'd never picked you up. I can see you've been telling the truth, and your employer speaks very highly of you. If it was up to me, I'd let you go, but it's too late, because the report's already been filed.'

'What does that mean?'

'You are charged with being *Exposed to Moral Danger* and you'll have to go to Winbirra Remand Centre for a couple of weeks until you go to court.'

I didn't need to ask about Winbirra. I'd heard about it from other girls when I was in Regent House. It had a reputation as a tough place, but at least I wasn't headed for Winlaton, which I knew was even worse.

'After you've been to court you'll be sent to a hostel, one like Regent House. Your boss said he'd hold your job for you so you'll be okay.'

She looked at me again, 'I really am sorry I picked you up, because I do believe you didn't know you were in a brothel. Just be more careful in the future about the company you keep.'

She drove me on the long drive out to Nunawading, stopping to buy me an ice cream on the way. This unexpected act of kindness raised my spirits and I thought things just might work out for me. After all, I still had a job and when I got into a hostel, I'd have a secure roof over my head. I could start again and life could be good.

Winbirra

Winbirra Remand Centre opened in 1960 as a holding place for young girls caught between police apprehension and a court-determined destination. It shared a common gateway with Winlaton Youth Training Centre, however, although part of the same parcel of land, the remand and youth training centres remained as separate entities. The address of Winbirra as 208 Springvale Road, while Winlaton itself was number 186. This demarcation between Winlaton and Winbirra was quite clear and any girl transferred to Winlaton from Winbirra would be recorded as a new admittance, the same as if she had come from any other facility. The division between the two centres was also evident in the layout of the site, once inside the Springvale Road entrance. Upon entering the driveway, the road divided at a small central lawn area and rose garden. Straight ahead was the administration block with the Winlaton compound behind it. The road to the south wound past Leawarra Hostel and on to Winbirra, skirting the barbed wire-topped corrugated iron wall of Winlaton. This defined Winbirra Remand and Leawarra Hostel as separate institutions, both carrying out distinctly different roles from the youth training centre.

The police car turned into the driveway at 186 Springvale Road and diverged to the left, passing an older style house, identified as Leawarra Hostel by a sign at the front of the building. The house looked warmly inviting, with its homely facade and plantings of yesteryear, but I hoped I wouldn't end up there. I'd heard about this place from girls who'd been in there, and those who hadn't but thought they knew anyway. All told stories of manipulation by staff and inmates and other horror tales.

Turning right, the road was over-shadowed by the perimeter wall of Winlaton Youth Training Centre. Eight foot high corrugated iron panels, topped with rows of barbed wire. I was relieved I wouldn't be going there. It had a reputation for brutality and gang rapes, and staff who took sadistic pleasure in implementing an exaggerated interpretation of the rules. Another large sign informed me I was now on the property of Winbirra Remand Centre, a division of the Department of Children's Welfare, a low-roofed structure at the rear of the Winlaton compound. Another corrugated iron fence, thematically capped with coils of barbed wire, abutted the end of the building. Windows, set with small square metal grilled panes, added to the starkness of the scene. The policewoman answered my look of apprehension by assuring me, once again, I only had to stay here for the couple of weeks it would take for the Children's Court to process me into a hostel. She pressed the bell with a familiarity of someone who'd been here often, and I heard the jangle of heavy keys approaching the door from the other side.

My transfer to the care and control of Winbirra took only seconds to complete and for the de-personalisation to begin. The policewomen were ushered from the building as I was steered unceremoniously down a long passage to an open shower area. Steam from a bath billowed and twirled towards ceiling vents in its escape from the overheated water. I wanted to merge with the steam, to billow and twirl my way out of this place, but my body had stalled into terrified numbness as the reality of my situation hit me. I was now an inmate. Two women in Terylene shirt-waist over-dresses, keys hanging from narrow belts, took turns to bark out instructions in thick English accents I could barely understand.

'Now coom along nar and get those cloothes off.'

'All of thoom nar and leave 'oom in a pile.'

I stared at them. Get my clothes off? Surely I wasn't expected to undress in front of them.

'Whootsa matter, shy are yoo? Too bad miss, thars noo pless fur moodesty aroon 'ere! Wi' seen it all afore an you aren't got nuthin different.'

They were losing patience with me.

'Nar miss...yoo doon't woont too get oof to a bad start do ya?'

'Coom on nar, let's be 'avin you in the bath nar.'

'We doon't put oop wi' trooblemakers aroon here.'

I knew there was no way out of it. I shucked off my clothes quickly, anxious to hide my nakedness under the water but, just as I was just about to step in the bath, I was told to stand still while they checked my body for marks or other distinguishing features.

'Any tattoos?'

'No.'

I stood in naked exposure, as one officer pored over my body and questioned the origin of every scar and flaw, while the other drew corresponding descriptions on a card. The burn scar on my leg looked surprisingly like a map of Tasmania. It should have comforted me but it made me homesick. My body was the hard data for their index file. Inspection over, I stepped quickly into the bath, grateful for its cover, but the heat of the water scalded my legs and my backside refused to sit. I stayed in a half squat position, arms folded across my breasts, willing my body to adjust to the heat.

'Nar sit darn and doon' be silly, a'm losin' patience with yoo.'

She pressed down hard on my shoulder until I slid into a sitting position. The water surged into my body cavities. It pulsed through the soft tissue of my vagina and seared its way across my belly, changing my skin colour to an angry pink. I was told to immerse my head under the water to wet my hair, before a cascade of Phenol disinfectant was poured over my head from a bottle held aloft.

It ran into my eyes.

It turned the bath water white and the pungent smell of its carbolic base took my breath away. I opened my mouth to breathe and it ran down my throat, burning and sucking the air from my lungs. I spluttered and gasped and the women laughed at their sport, all the while speaking their strange language.

'Woosh your har and then woosh yoursel' all oova an mek sure you clean under your arms an atween your laigs.'

A cracked bar of Velvet soap hit my elbow and sank to the bottom of the tub. I chased it around and through my bent legs, before I succeeded in trapping it against the heavy chain secured to the plug.

Slivers of soap flaked off in my hair, as I tried in vain to get work it into lather, snarled in the hard tangle of my effort.

Once they were satisfied I'd been sufficiently disinfected, I was ordered out of the bath and handed a rough towel. White, with a red stripe on either end, *Property of the Victorian Government* marked in large, irregular letters along the edge. My wet hair, cold now I'd moved away from the blanket of toxic steam, dripped disconsolately down my back. I quickly put on the clothes they handed to me, ignoring the dampness of my body in my eagerness to cover myself.

A bra and cotton underpants, both well-worn and misshapen, had a single word scrawled on the stretched bands of each, 'Winbirra'. This classification was repeated on the remaining items of clothing: a shirt and skirt, white cotton socks and a pair of sandshoes. Before I was allowed to put the socks on, *mercurochrome* was applied liberally between my toes, with cotton wool twirled around a match thin splinter of wood; the socks permanently marked with a red slash across the white. I was handed a toothbrush. A dob of toothpaste sat in the valley of the bristles, blunted and pointing sideways from punishment by previous users. This item had escaped the black indelible marking pen, but ownership could still be identified by the section name inscribed into the handle. My depersonalisation was almost complete.

One of the women attacked my hair with a nit comb, in a simian-like search for head lice. She jerked my head sharply, as the discoloured pink teeth pulled against the small pieces of soap trapped in the tangle of my hair. Finally, exhausted by her effort, or convinced my hair was free of vermin, she released me. I was instructed to take the clothes I'd been wearing to a laundry area, handed another bar of Velvet soap and pointed in the direction of a wash trough. Just like home, Velvet soap was used for everything in this place from bathing, washing dishes, hand-washing clothes to household cleaning, but with Phenol as an additive.

I followed their every instruction in a daze. This wasn't happening to me. It couldn't be. A few hours ago I'd had my freedom, going about the difficult business of surviving, and now the person I'd been had ceased to exist. As much as I'd always wished I could step into another life, this certainly wasn't what I'd had in mind. But it was happening and the reality of this was brought home to me when a heavy door was unlocked and I viewed the outside area for the first time. Escorted and supervised while I hung my dripping clothes on the line, the only structure in the compound, an expanse of weed-invested grass enclosed by the vertical corrugated iron walls of the boundary fence that towered high above me. I looked at the lines of barbed wire strung tightly between metal pipes, bolted into a vee shape, with more coils of barbed wire balanced between the strands, and wondered how anyone might escape from this place.

It was a prison.

I was almost a Winbirra girl. I only had to be interviewed by the head of section before my induction was complete. Another buxom pom, in another Terylene frock worn over street clothes with the obligatory bunch of keys at her waist, told me the rules and expectations of the place. She had the attitude of one who only ever expected the worst of people, her words held an under-current of menace and she punctuated her speech with details of the consequences for non-compliance with the rules. Interrupting her spiel, she picked up my right hand and turned it palm up, as evidence of my uselessness.

'I can see these hands have never done a day's work. We'll soon fix that.'

I decided against answering her. She'd already showed her level of intelligence with this statement and didn't appear the type to hear anyone else's point of view.

I knew the next step would be to meet the other inmates and I was anxious for this to be over, uneasy about what lay behind the locked door at the end of the passage. I hoped I wouldn't be called upon to prove myself in any way, as I had no intention of getting involved in other people's concerns. I was only going to be here for two weeks, or less if I went to court earlier, and I had nothing to prove to anyone.

The officer looked through the long glass slot in the door, a wary look on her face, before inserting the key and pushing the door inward. Girls sat around the room in groups of twos and threes. They wore the same scrubbed clean look, but their toughness showed through in their body language and facial expressions. Then the door closed behind me and I was left with the pack, who sniffed me from a distance, before deciding I was no immediate threat to the social order, and proceeded to tell me how the place really operated. They competed with each other to ask me questions about myself, why I'd been put in Winbirra and where I'd be going next. There was no excitement in my story. I answered in monosyllables and didn't try to elaborate on it.

The days disappeared in a fog of regimentation. Every minute of the day planned with such inviolable precision, it was difficult not to breach some minor regulation. There were no requests and no agreeable instruction from task to perform the most perfunctory of tasks, only orders barked in the difficult to decipher English accent I'd already grown to despise. It didn't matter whether anyone understood a rule or order, or whether it made sense or not, any questioning by the inmates was viewed as noncompliance.

Each morning began with the sound of a hand banging flat-palmed on the metal door, and a disembodied voice telling me to get up, make my bed and sweep the floor. Once this had been done to the satisfaction of the officer, who surveyed the room economically through the narrow viewing pane, while I remained standing at attention by the side of my bed, the door was unlocked, my day clothes from where I'd left them the night before, folded neatly outside my door, and I was escorted to the bathroom area. Here I showered in a door-less cubicle under the watchful eyes of the staff.

After showering and dressing, we were taken to the recreation room and locked in until our names were called, and we lined up along the passage to have our clothes checked for conformity. No skirts were to be rolled over at the waist to shorten them, socks had to be folded down neatly, and our hair combed into a cloned style of every other girl.

Any attempt at individuality, no matter how minor, was recorded as a breach of rules. Inspection over, we were marched into the dining room where red and white checked table cloths brought some relief to the greyness of the rubberised floor covering and the gloss painted walls. An officer stood at rigid attention by the locked door at all times.

Meals were cooked in bulk in the central kitchen at Winlaton and transported down in portable Bain Maries, referred to as hot boxes. It was ordinary fare, with high carbohydrate blandness, but it divided the day into recognisable segments that helped pass time. Food played a major role in any institution, as it was often the only diversion to look forward to each day. Cold toast and a scraping of butter and a bowl of thin salted porridge, eaten after a long night in isolation, was indeed food for the spirit.

On the rare occasions we were taken outside for exercise, we were made to jog around the inside perimeter of the compound, while staff barked commands from the comfort of the porch area. Most days, however, we remained indoors, spending the hours between mealtimes locked in the recreation room, a large rectangular space with bench seats fitted to the walls. There were no books to read and newspapers and radios were not allowed, so inmates just sat around and talked. This often led to disagreements and fights, where frustration and futility gave power to fists and feet and teeth. No Queensberry rules in this place.

Some of the girls liked to brag about their exploits, whether criminal or sexual, and they ran to a different set of values than mine. There was no escape from this room, nor the behaviour and conversations that took place within it and there were those who used this to advance their own sexual satisfaction. Deprivation, and how to ease this, was always a popular topic that occasionally led to girls engaging in open masturbation. The staff came irregularly to look through the slot, but there were a number of blind spots in the room and everyone was well aware of where they were. I turned away from the spectacle of girls rutting against the legs of furniture, ashamed to be female and the degradation I'd been reduced to.

Apart from mealtimes, and the ritual line-ups along the passage, the only other distractions were when a new girl arrived, if someone left to go to court, or waiting to see if anyone visited on a weekend. New arrivals were always welcomed for news they might bring from the outside world. They'd be interrogated as to whom they knew and what they'd done, and their responses changed the dynamics of the group. If a girl presented as timid or slow, she'd immediately became the scapegoat for pent up anger and emotion of the more aggressive personalities. If she showed herself to be street wise and tough, she was accepted immediately into the upper echelon of the hierarchy although she'd be challenged upon to prove herself at some stage.

There was an air of mystery attached to any court appearance. On the day in question the girls concerned would be kept apart from the rest of the section, a precaution against messages getting in or out of the centre, but where there's a will, there will always be a way, and many a girl left the centre with small pieces of paper concealed in or about her body. Most messages, however, were given verbally, and the poor girl going out was expected to remember multiple names and phone numbers, addresses, times and places, but it was all part of the game of diversion. The majority of these messages became forgotten the minute the door clanged shut, or discarded with the first flush of the toilet at the Children's Court.

Nobody ever knew what fate awaited them ahead of a court appearance. Sometimes a girl would return as a re-remand, other times there'd be a temporary return for a few days until a hostel or some other placement was finalized. On very rare occasions, they might be given another chance by the court and allowed to return to their family. On court day, a police divisional van would pick up those scheduled for appearance, stopping first at Winbirra then proceeding to Winlaton to pick up inmates from there.

The day of my court appearance finally arrived and it was my turn to go through the exit ritual. I had no contact with other inmates and remained in my room until after they'd been to the showers and had their breakfast. Taken to the laundry room, I was handed the large paper bag my own clothes had been stored in and told to iron them to wear to court. After showering, I dressed in my own clothes, a civilizing effect after the shapeless section garments.

When the police arrived I had to sign for a return of my other belongings; one purse and its contents, which had to be counted to ensure it tallied with the admission entry. Two of us went to court from Winbirra that day. I only ever knew the other girl by her nickname, 'Boof'. She was tall, pear shaped, with lank straight hair that hung in strands over her freckled brow. She didn't look like a girl who'd had a lot of opportunity to get into trouble, not the kind of trouble that came from boys anyway, which appeared to be at the base of every other girl's problems. She was friendly though, and I felt comforted by her large presence in the back of the van, particularly when we stopped at Winlaton to pick up more girls.

I heard them before the van door swung open and they were thrown in by the escorting police. There were only three girls, but they filled the small space with their anger and curses and a simmering threat of violence. Two sat close together on the narrow bench seats that ran down each side of the enclosure, feet braced against the metal ribs of the floor, as the vehicle accelerated out of the driveway and turned into Springvale Road. I was to learn this was a favourite sport for young police officers, who found humour in spilling their human cargo onto the floor and an involuntary acrobatic display. One girl had blonde hair, combed into an Elvis style ducktail bodgie haircut, which was in direct contrast to the femininity of her dress. If I'd had any doubt about her sexual orientation, this disappeared when she embraced her partner and the two began to kiss, long and passionately. They only came up for air once, when the masculine-looking girl snarled at me, her lip styled in the famous Presley sneer.

'Whatta ya fucken lookin' at? Haven' ya seen a fucken lezo before?'

It was only then I realized I'd been staring, mesmerised by the scene before me.

It was a long drive from Nunawading to the Children's Court in Batman Avenue. I disappeared inside myself as I contemplated the outcome of the day, hoping I'd be sent to Regent House, or released into my boss's care. I'd be happy to go almost anywhere except back where I'd just come from.

The brown linoleum floored passage of the children's court was packed with police officers, men in suits, white-faced kids, and careworn mothers. I was escorted to a holding room at the end of the passage, the police officer holding tight to the waistband of my slacks causing me to walk with a stiff legged, tiptoed gait. I tried to look around at the crowd as we moved down the long corridor, hoping to see someone I knew, but there were only strangers to return my stare. Everyone wore the same look of bewilderment at the constant bustle and movement of people. From time to time, the door of the holding room opened to admit a solicitor, who'd engage in a rapidly whispered consultation, before scuttling out again. One by one, the occupants of the room were called into the various courtrooms. Some returned after a while, looking dejected or defiant, eyes bright with the unshed tears of rejection. The room would buzz as others sought information from them and distraction from their own worries.

'Whadya get?'

'D'ya 'ave to go back?'

'Fucken bastards!'

I didn't join in any of this conversation. I didn't belong here and I wasn't one of them. I didn't want to think about anything except being released from this nightmare and finally my name was called.

'Merlene Fawdry to court room two. Merlene Fawdry to court room two.'

The familiar tug on the back of my pants steered me through the waiting throng. In the small courtroom, I stood when I was told to stand

and sat when told to take a seat. I looked up at the magistrate hopefully and lowered my eyes again when I saw myself reflected in his gaze. My pink slacks had taken on a disrespectful brightness in the drab brown of the room and my gold shoes winked provocatively. Discussion rumbled around me and he addressed a female court official seated somewhere behind me.

'Is there any word from the girl's parents?'

'No, your honour.'

He shuffled his papers, harrumphed loudly, and then spoke again.

'Remanded to Winbirra Remand Centre for a further two weeks, pending a report from her parents.'

I was ushered from the court in a state of shock. Two weeks. I'd be in Winbirra for another two weeks. I couldn't believe it and I was still trying to comprehend what had happened when I arrived back at the centre. I could feel a simmering anger, born of yet another betrayal. I'd been told I'd only have to stay two weeks in the first place, and here I was, back for another two. Nobody had spoken with me about my situation, my presence at court had been as silent witness to discussions concerning my life, and the decision had been made by strangers; people who only knew me by the reports provided by other strangers.

I was inducted back into Winbirra using the only regulatory process allowed. Sign in, strip, disinfect and bath. Check body for any new marks that might have emerged within the past few hours. Mercurochrome between the toes and presentation of yet another used toothbrush. I suppose they didn't want me to get attached to anything, or to feel a sense of belonging. It was, after all, only a remand centre. I washed my clothes, hung them out to dry and returned to the recreation room. It all seemed so pointless. I began to have a greater empathy with the other girls now, joining in with their bullshit and idle gossip.

The next Sunday provided a welcome break when Marcia came to visit. She was shocked and upset at my appearance, and with my incarceration in this place. I put on a tough front, as I'd been doing since my return from court. It was the number one rule for survival, as to let anyone how I really felt would expose my vulnerability. It didn't matter anyway. Marcia couldn't help me get out of the place. She was moving on to Sydney in a few days. I asked her about my belongings left behind at the squat, which was everything that I owned in the world, and she promised to see they were safe and let me know where I could pick them up from when I got out.

Observing movements in and out of Winbirra, I noted that girls I expected to be sent to Winlaton after they'd attended court, those who'd acted the toughest, boasted the loudest and who used the crudest language, often went home or on to softer placements. Then there were other girls I never expected to see return from court, who'd been caught in the institutional trap. Nice quiet girls, whose only legal contravention was in having parents who were unable or unwilling to care for them, or those charged with being *Exposed to moral danger*. Many of these girls had lived in institutions and foster care for most of their lives, often being moved on because they rebelled against acts of abuse against them. Children and young people had no say in where they lived and no credibility when it came to making allegations against an adult. The injustice of their position in life fuelled the fire of social consciousness in my belly that would grow with the years and until the opportunity to address the imbalance of power presented itself in adulthood.

It was an unforgiving and inequitable system and, within the care system of Winbirra, there was no solace or sympathy for any. The majority of the staff were British immigrants, recruited direct from the nearby migrant hostel, with no training or true vocation for this type of work and following the Borstal model of their home country. There were no words of kindness and no interest shown in our lives. These workers remained detached from the needs of the inmates and I polished the same veneer of indifference.

The return trip back to children's court at the end of the two weeks was an exercise in déjà vu. I knew the routine by now, the reversed intake procedure and the re-personalisation as I put on my clothes. I said my goodbyes and made arrangements to catch up with girls I'd made friends with once I was established in a hostel somewhere, knowing as I spoke I had no intention of doing this.

The procedure inside the courtroom was different this time. When the magistrate asked if there was any word from my parents, the voice behind me spoke up clearly.

'Yes, your Honour. We've spoken to the girl's mother and she definitively doesn't want any more to do with her.'

I didn't take in the rest of the discussion, a low rumbling of importance as decisions were made about my life. I'd always known she hadn't wanted me, but it was still something of a shock to have it said aloud by other people. Eventually the magistrate looked up and addressed a point behind my left ear. His words ran into one another and my mind only absorbed the edge of it.

'...order that...Ward of the State of Victoria ...placed in a hostel.'

I was taken into an office for an interview with a social worker, the first and last contact I had with any professional welfare officer. She talked to me about what I'd like to happen with my life, without listening to any reply I made. She told me my case had been adjourned the previous fortnight because she'd had difficulty contacting my mother. When she'd finally managed to speak with her, my mother had made it clear she wanted nothing more to do with me. I was out of her life forever.

The social worker told me she was looking for a hostel placement for me and I'd have to go back to Winbirra for the week or two it would take to arrange this. I wasn't too pleased about going back, but I felt at least I was making progress, someone had spoken to me about what was happening. Apart from being locked up, which I knew I'd never get used to, I was familiar with the remand centre routine. I could last two more weeks if it meant my life would eventually be my own and I settled back into the regimentation of the centre, counting down the days to freedom.

I'd counted three days and had just fallen asleep on the eve of the fourth, when I was woken by a pounding on my door.

'Wakey, wakey. Let's be 'aven you then.'

I was slow to wake, disoriented by the change in the regimented system I'd become used to. The light turned on and bit into my eyes as I struggled to open them. The key jangled and clunked in the lock, and the door thrown open.

'Come on then, 'op to it. You're goin' for a ride.'

The person behind the voice yanked the bed covers off and threw a tattered candlewick dressing gown at me.

'Come on now. Mrs Somersett's waitin' for yer an she hasn't got all night.'

Once was out in the passage I could see I wasn't alone. Boof stood there in the same sleepy disarray, thin dressing gown stretched across her square hips. I knew what was happening, because I'd heard it happen on other nights to other girls. It was the night transfer to Winlaton.

There'd been a mistake. I knew Boof had been sentenced to Winlaton, but I hadn't. I was going to a hostel. The magistrate had told me this. The social worker had told me this.

A very tall woman stood at the admission desk, short curly hair and an angular face that hinted of a spiteful temperament. Her thin lips snapped commands. This was Mrs Somersett, the deputy head of Winlaton.

'I'm not meant to be going to Winlaton. I'm going to a hostel.'

At the sound of my voice, she whipped her head in my direction.

'You'll go where we send you, miss. You don't make the rules around here.'

She attempted to silence me with a fixed stare from her ice blue eyes, as she advanced towards me.

'The magistrate told me I'd be...'

'I don't care who told you what. You're going to Winlaton. Tonight!'

She grabbed my arm and thrust me towards the door as she ordered staff to unlock it. Boof followed us meekly into the frosty night air, where an open topped jeep stood a few yards from the door. Two large German Shepherd dogs sat upright in the passenger seats. I balked again at the sight of the dogs, but Mrs Somersett pushed me closer to the jeep, her knuckles sharp through the worn fabric of my robe as she ordered me to get in. The dogs growled in reaction to the anger in her voice, eyeing me off as the cause. Boof sensed my fear and attempted to get in the jeep first so I wouldn't have to sit next to the dog in the back seat, but Mrs Somersett recognised both my fear and the ploy, ordering Boof to stand back while I took my place next to the agitated dog. It's low snarl and bared teeth reinforced my terror, as its mistress admonished it to sit.

The moon reflected off the corrugated walls of the compound as she drove me towards my new home.

Winlaton

In 1956, Winlaton Juvenile School opened to deal with the broadening category of female juvenile delinquents; girls who attracted police and welfare attention for being potentially delinquent and for behaviour related to their socio-economic circumstances or non-criminal behaviour. Known officially as Winlaton Youth Training Centre, it was established on an eighteen-acre plot of land off Springvale Road, Nunawading, which had been named 'Winlaton' after the English town of a former owner's birth. The rural setting of the farm was maintained, and the old weatherboard farmhouse, 'Winlaton', was later renamed Leawarra and used to accommodate select reformed residents on release from the training centre.

Senior staff, particularly the section chiefs, had discretion to mete out punishment to the girls on their section. They were not allowed to deny food or physically touch the girls, although solitary confinement could be used to allow a girl to calm down away from other girls and staff. Solitary confinement was not a separate section of Winlaton, so much as an allocated room on each section.

Following a return from absconding, girls were placed in secure isolation in Goonyah section to prevent immediate re-absconding. From Goonyah, they could earn their way onto the more open sections of Warrina and Karingal and, between 1960 and 1964, to Leawarra. For smaller misdemeanours such as swearing at staff or smoking, which was forbidden, individual officers could enforce some forms of punishment. Again, this was necessary because waiting until the morning or until a senior staff was available would remove the immediacy and relevance of reprimand for breaches.

The jeep pulled up outside the administration block of Winlaton and Mrs Somersett led us through a series of doors, unlocking and relocking each as we passed into the area beyond. The last door opened onto a concrete courtyard and, beyond this, I could see the security lights of the oval, around which the three residential sections of the institution had been built. A halo of fog surrounded each spotlight and a low mist swept the ground. The dogs had settled down now they were back in their more familiar patrol zone and they padded ahead to a building at the top of the compound, sniffing the air for trouble.

The path we followed led to a long, low brick structure, built in the same style as Winbirra, with the same small-paned windows set in square metal grills. Mrs Somersett selected an over-sized key to unlock a metal gate at the side of the section. This opened inward onto a porch; the floor covered with square tiles the colour of damp earth. This was the mud room, a decontamination zone between the natural elements outside and the pristine cleanliness of the section. She relocked the mud room gate before unlocking the next door, which took us straight into the dimly lit lobby of the building itself.

This was Goonyah, the security section of Winlaton.

I'd first heard about this place when I was in Regent House and more recently, Winbirra. It was the section where new arrivals were held until they'd been through the full intake and assessment process, and while they acclimatised to life behind a barbed wire fence. It was also the section where the worst behaved girls were kept: the mad, the bad and the sad, the habitual absconders, and those who retained an independent spirit. I'd heard tales of bashings by staff and gang rapes by inmates, and of clandestine sexual encounters with the gate-men for the price of a cigarette. I was terrified of what lay in wait for me behind its locked doors.

Goonyah was quiet at this hour. The inmates had been locked in their rooms for the night and the dimmed lights of the long, brick walled passage added to the gloomy atmosphere. The passage had many doors placed at regular intervals on either side and I could see each of them had the standard viewing slot set in the centre. We were greeted by two women wearing the same style Terylene uniforms as Winbirra staff, and the same large ring of keys hanging from their belts. One took our transfer papers, while the other one handed us a flannelette nightgown each, locking us in separate rooms to change our clothes.

The key clicked in the lock as the door closed behind me. There was no door handle and the only adornment was the vertical observation slot. Red brick walls, a single bed, and bare wooden floorboards. The metal grilled window looked out onto the oval of grass I'd passed on the way in. Keeping one eye on the slot in the door, I changed out of my clothes quickly, pulling the nightie over my head before I took off the Winbirra clothing I'd been wearing. I felt vulnerable standing there, conscious of my nakedness beneath the outsized nightdress, as the cold air crept under its loose folds and clung to my body. Goosebumps of fear refused to be silenced by the touch of the rough fabric against my skin. Once I'd changed I crossed to the window and looked out at the grounds of my new home. Beyond the towering security lights, I could make out the top of the fence, its barbed wire silhouetted against the night sky: a lonely study in black, white and grey.

'Get away from that window!'

I jumped in fright and turned to see someone looking at me through the slot before it was opened by an officer, who retrieved the garments I'd taken off. She told me again to stay away from the window and get into bed; the rules would be explained to me by the section chief in the morning.

The sheets were stiff with cold and starch, slippery white cardboard that gave off the same smell of Phenol I'd been showered in that first day in Winbirra. I pushed the bedclothes away from my face to escape from the suffocating fumes, exposing the top half of my body to the cold. The toxic blend surrounded me and took my breath away, but there was no escape. Then room went dark and I realized the light switch, as with the doorknob, was on the passage side of the door. Like everything else in my life, it was outside of my control. The lights on the oval shone through the uncurtained window, the shadow of the grill imprinted across the brick wall near my head. Bars against brick walls. It was a grim reminder of where I was and tears of self-pity, my old enemy, pushed against the back of my eyes but before I could release them, the room flooded with light again. I looked towards the door and saw a face looking back at me. One eye, anyway. I was on show, a curiosity. I was glad I'd stopped the tears before they began because I didn't want anyone to see weakness from me, or to think I cared about anything. Emotional detachment had served me well in the past and this, and a tough attitude, would be my tools to survival in this place.

I heard an authoritative voice from further up the passage order the eye away from my door and the light went out once again. I looked at the pattern on the wall, the sinister outline of the window against the starkness of the bricks, and I closed my heart to any emotion except hatred. I let the feeling run over and through me, feeling the power of it, and I fed it with memories of past hurts and rejections.

I'd been put in this place of punishment for no reason.

I'd been lied to by everybody I'd come in contact with.

All my life people had used me as an outlet for their own emotions and frustrations and I'd accepted that as all I deserved. I'd been too afraid to speak out and too timid to stand up for myself. I'd thought if I made myself invisible I'd be protected from attack. If I was patient and well-behaved and smiled long enough, my real mother would take me away from all that was wrong in my life. I knew now this was never going to happen.

She'd given birth to me and then just as quickly given me away. She hadn't wanted me, any more than anyone else who'd come into my life and she was never coming back.

I hated her and I hated all mothers.

I was in this place for the moment, but I was going to survive, no matter what I had to do. They could clank their keys and lock me up. They could depersonalise me and make me a clone of every girl in here, but I knew they'd never reach the place deep inside where my spirit dwelt.

The lights around the oval gave way to the grey dawn and the institution came to life, a non-stop clank of keys, as doors were locked and unlocked. I heard the mutterings of waking voices. Early morning voices of the staff, freshly rasped from pre-shift cigarettes, rose above and around the expletive laden protests from girls who preferred to stay in bed. I listened and tried to make out the routine, hoping it might save any misunderstanding of the rules later on. I'd already worked out only one girl was allowed out of their bedroom and taken to the shower at a time, when I was ordered to strip and remake my bed while I waited for my turn. A broom and scrubbing brush were passed through the door and I was ordered to sweep and then dry scrub the floor, to make the floorboards shine. The door closed again.

When my turn came to be unlocked, I found a bra and underpants hanging on the outside handle of my door, both ill-fitting cotton garments of generic size. I was handed the green and white check shirt and grey skirt with a ticking stripe that added another layer of uniformity. White cotton socks were piled against one wall to be distributed after the mercurochrome had been painted between our toes. The only belongings of personal ownership allowed were a plastic comb and a toothbrush, unused this time, which were given out from the store to all new girls. I was told if either of these needed to be replaced at any time they'd have to be purchased from my pocket money.

After I'd showered and dressed, I was locked with the other inmates in a communal room separated from the staff duty office by a window of toughened glass. Officially known as the small recreation room, it was more commonly called the rec room or small rec. It had an empty fireplace at one end and a grilled window along the wall opposite the staff-viewing window. Under the grilled window was the only piece of furniture in the room, a wooden box seat that had neither cushions, nor other covering. The brick wall theme of the section continued into this

35

room, although, in a facile concession to ordinariness, the top two feet of the wall had been faced with plaster. The names of inmates past and present, along with the dates of their incarceration and sentiments about the place had been etched deeply into this section of this wall.

The office window had several sheets of paper taped to the office side. One was a long list of section rules, which, I was to learn the hard way, were subject to interpretation between staff members. A job roster demonstrated the ever-changing Goonyah population, as it used room numbers in place of names and next to this was a list of room numbers showing the names of the current occupants.

I was number two. The last sheet was a list of room numbers for each meal sitting. There were fifteen beds in the section and sixteen chairs in the dining room, but no more than eight girls were allowed to be in the dining room at any one time. Goonyah girls were considered to be intractable and dangerous and not to be trusted to have natural interaction with each other when present in large numbers.

One by one, the girls were ushered into the rec room, belligerent through habit and conformity to expected behaviour. Freshly combed damp hair, framed each shiny face, fresh with youth, yet etched deeply with rejection and hopelessness. Arms and legs displayed institution tattoos, crosses, daggers, and scrolls that framed the word 'Mum', while here and there a small rose bloomed between the raised scars of self-mutilation. The conflict between love and hate spelt out in thick uneven lettering on fingers scarcely old enough to know about either. The pain of life was evident in all.

There was only enough space for five girls to sit on the bench seat and the rest had to either stand or sit on the floor, with its unwelcome marbled rubberised floor covering. If any sought personal space on the viewing window side of the room, a tap from the office side of the glass came as a quick reminder to move back to where they could be seen.

The introduction of new girls was similar to Winbirra; the staring off and sniffing out, and questions asked in an aggressive manner. I was aware my status as a new girl placed me at the bottom of the pecking order, and of the need to establish myself quickly if I didn't want to be the target of every other girl's frustration, for however long I was going to be in this place. I turned my fear into front, my apprehension into false courage, and I returned their stares. I responded to questions asked in an overly aggressive manner, with silence and steady eye contact. I analysed the group dynamics to ascertain who the key players were and I played only to them. This approach worked for the moment and the predators turned their attention to easier targets.

The staff on Goonyah also shared the attitudes of their Winbirra counterparts. The chief of the section, Mrs Eliot, introduced herself to me while the first sitting was at breakfast. She had a thin line where her mouth was supposed to be, and spoke in a clipped tone as she outlined the rules I was to live by. True to the culture of the institution, she spoke as if she expected me to break the rules, as if I'd already broken some sacred trust and my presence in this place meant I'd forfeited the right to be treated with any sort of respect or dignity. She reminded me of my mother.

There was no reason given as to why any of the rules were in place and, while I understood some were necessary for health and safety within the section, many seemed to have no sound basis at all. It was one of these I'd already unwittingly broken, when I looked out the window the previous night. I was told if I was caught doing it again, I'd be transferred to the other side of the building, with its unchanging view of the security fence. I didn't understand what difference this would make if I wasn't allowed to look out of the window anyway but kept my opinion to myself. She explained the pocket money system to me. I could earn up to four shillings a week, enabling me to place an order at the canteen to buy sweets or a comb or a toothbrush. However, money could also be deducted for any misdemeanour. It was the same give with one hand, take with the other, I'd experienced in the convent. The invisible pocket money.

Once the first sitting had finished their meal and the girls secured in the rec room, it was my turn to line up with the second sitting. We stood in a row against the passage wall, left arm held straight out and touching on the shoulder of the girl in front. This regimented measure of distance had to be maintained while our clothing was checked for uniformity and general tidiness. The biggest irritation for the chief appeared to be the sight of a girl with her socks pulled up, instead of a neat double fold that exposed the back of the ankle. An offence of this nature could result in loss of pocket money, as could an untucked shirt, untidy hair, or anything else that caught her eye. It didn't take much to offend her.

After breakfast we were taken from the rec room, one at a time, to do our allocated jobs. No one genuinely complained about this, as it allowed a temporary break from the discomfort of the small room, but the obligatory protests had to be maintained. The jobs were menial and gratuitous. The linoleum floor of the long passage had to be dry-scrubbed twice a day, kept to a high shine nobody except the staff and inmates ever saw. Toilets and showers were on the daily cleaning list and the smell of phenol permeated every part of the building. The most sought after job was kitchen duty, because this was shared with another girl, and provided opportunity for almost normal conversation.

The remainder of the day was spent in the small and inappropriately named recreation room. Fifteen girls and their pent up emotions, from a lifetime of rejection and deprivation, sandwiched into a small room for hours on end. There was nothing to break the tedium of these hours. We were not allowed to have anything to read and there was no craftwork. If the staff felt inclined, they'd flick a switch in the office, channelling the radio through a speaker in the ceiling and we could listen to a station of their choosing. They were meticulous in the administration of their duties though and always muted the speaker before the news came on. I was told the reason for this rule was that they didn't want anyone to hear something from the 'outside' that might upset them. For the entire period of our incarceration, we were kept ignorant of events in the world beyond the wall. The speaker privilege was often used by staff for their own reasons, to break their own boredom, and they would turn it down low at the beginning of a song they knew to be a favourite. I couldn't work out if this was just to get a reaction, or if the staff also liked to flex their muscles for the new girls.

'Turn it up!'

The chorus began, ignored by staff until it reached a crescendo that could no longer be ignored.

'Turn it up, ya bitch!'

Feet stamped and fists clashed with the metal door and the toughened glass, which bounced under the impact. The smirks fell off the faces in the duty office and staff came at a run to the rec room door, knuckles hidden behind the metal cage of their keys. The ringleaders were removed, subdued by covert dustings from those same keys, and the punishment announced.

'There'll be no radio for the rest of the day for that, girls.'

And we were left to entertain ourselves or to be entertained by the speech and actions of others.

On the first day of my admission, there was competition to impress Boof and me, the new girls. There was much talk about absconding and, as returned runaways were re-housed in Goonyah, there were a couple of girls who could lay claim to escaping. It was these inmates who commanded the greatest admiration. They had nothing more to prove. Boof won instant acceptance because of her size and height. She was told she'd make a good *bunker* as these were always in short supply; a lifetime of poor institution diet and other deprivations meant many of the girls were short in statue and of slight build.

When someone wanted to abscond, a strong tall girl was required to stand with her back against the fence, her hands linked in front of her. From this position she bunked girls up as they placed one foot in the cupped hands, to climb up on her shoulders, the only way to reach the bottom of the metal vee section that formed the cradle for the coils of barbed wire. The pipe would be grasped in both hands, while the climber walked her feet up the corrugated iron wall, and then moved hand over hand until she was holding the end of the vee section. From this position, she could climb through the strands on barbed wire and wind her way through the coils to the outer vee. Here the action was reversed, except there was no bunker standing outside to ease the journey down. The only way down on the other side was to drop from the metal pipe, without snagging on the wire or the deep serrated edges of the corrugated iron, and to land without breaking a limb. There were stories told of arms and legs cut open to the bone, and several girls wore the scars to attest to this, and tales of broken limbs. It was easy to see that anyone who got away deserved some fame and recognition. Boof was booked weeks in advance and she played the game beautifully, becoming an instant friend to the hard-core mob. Lucky Boof.

There were two girls on the section in the last months of pregnancy. They wore smock dresses made in the sewing room by girls from the open sections. Poorly made and badly fitting, these dresses added to their look of discomfort. Dresses of shame for reluctant little mothers. There was no dispensation made for their condition by staff or inmates. They sat on the wooden seat if they managed to get a seat or on the floor like the rest of us if they didn't, and no one was interested in their complaints. Apart from admiring the exploits of the most daring, there was no other respect shown in this place, least of all self-respect.

My first day passed in a series of line-ups, meals eaten under the watchful eyes of two staff that stood, one in each corner, and acted as guardians of good manners, and hours spent in the rec room. Anyone needing to use the toilet had to attract the attention of the staff in the duty office and request to be unlocked and escorted. Often the staff ignored these requests, in favour of continuing their own conversations, and the situation became desperate.

'Let me out for a piss.'

'D'ya wanna see me shit meself?'

'Let me out ya fucken moll!'

40

The latter never ceased to get attention. The door would be unlocked and the offender removed to the toilet, and then locked in her room as punishment for swearing.

At eight-thirty each evening, we were taken from the rec room two at a time, and locked in our rooms to take off our clothes and put on our nighties. Unlocked again and taken to the laundry room, we hand washed our socks, bra and knickers with velvet soap, placing them on a rack in the gas fired clothes drier. Our shoes, shirt, and skirt were folded neatly and placed outside our door. A minute squirt of toothpaste was put on our brush and, after cleaning our teeth and using the toilet, we were locked in our room again until the next morning.

On my second night in Goonyah, I lay between the stiff carbolic scented sheets, cold under the thin blankets, and reflected on the day.

I was still in one piece.

I hadn't been assaulted and, while I deplored the undertones of violence and the quiet rage it generated within its occupants, I realized I was now very much a part of it.

Days passed, each one a replica of the one before it. The only variation was in new girls admitted and others transferred to other sections. Faceless girls. Green and white checked shirts. Ticking skirts. Folded down socks lined up along the passage an arms width apart, distinguishable from each other only by size and strength and colour of language, which eventually painted us all in the same shade of muck.

Goonyah. My training ground for survival.

I met Mrs Somersett again when she strode into the section one day, a swarm of one, and ordered the staff to take us outside for exercise. This was the first time since my admission all of the girls had been out of the rec room at the one time. We lined up, unhitched our skirts, folded down our socks, and marched up the passage, arms attached to shoulders, to a wide metal door of a room unimaginatively called the big rec. This was a cavernous room marked out as a basketball court, and it carried the décor theme of polished board floors and uncurtained

41

grilled windows I'd become used to. Originally intended for use as a recreation area when the weather was inclement and the enclosed exercise yard behind the section could not be accessed, it was never used for the purpose intended.

At the far side of this room was another metal door that opened onto the grassy verge of a netball court. Here we were directed to sit in a group. I could see girls from the other sections gathered at the side of the court. Their clothes differed from the Goonyah girls by the variety of colour and dress style that, although institutional, that allowed for some individuality.

Mrs Somersett selected girls to form a team and I was relieved not to be chosen. Ball games were not my forte. I was uncoordinated at the best of times, but more so when under pressure, and I felt under pressure as I sat in the weak sun, and oddly vulnerable outside the brick walls I'd become used to. Girls from the other sections stared as they sized up the new girls. Out in the open air they looked larger, tougher, their arms stained with institution tattoo, and faces stained with survival. I shrank into the grass and whispered to the girl next to me.

'I'm glad she didn't pick me to play.'

It was only a whisper from one girl to another, but it reached the ears of Mrs Somersett who stood, arms folded against her flat chest, some distance away. She turned her icy eyes in my direction and yelled through the megaphone of her mean lips.

'Who's not going to play?'

I lowered my head and played dumb, but her voice came closer.

'WHO said they're NOT going to PLAY?'

She was now standing over me. I had to answer. I wanted to repeat the words I'd whispered, but all eyes were upon me, all ears attuned to the silence. I lifted my head and looked hard into Mrs Somersett's eyes. I knew it didn't matter what I said, she'd still interpret it as non-compliance. There was a satisfaction in meeting her eyes, however.

'I said I'm glad I didn't get picked to play.'

The ice in her eyes turned to glint as I recognised my mother in this woman. I sensed this was a stand-off and the break would not be good.

'STAND UP!'

This was it. The first salvo of the war.

My legs locked in place and refused the order to stand. I never took my eyes off her face and I failed to see her arm as it flew towards my head. She grabbed my hair on the downward swoop and continued her hold as she raised her arm. My body lifted, my head involuntarily following my hair as it threatened to separate from my scalp. My feet dangled above the ground and I swung like a rag doll as, with her free hand, she slapped me repeatedly across the face.

'Don't you tell me what you will or won't do!'

I kept my eyes on her the whole time. Hers cold and sadistic and mine filled with hatred. She threw me onto the court and motioned to another girl to get off.

'Now play!'

I could feel the stares and hear the whispers, but I was beyond caring. I stood where I'd landed at the edge of the court without moving. I made no effort to intercept the ball when it came in my direction and ignored the calls from the other players.

'Catch the fucken ball ya fucken stooge.'

To be called a stooge was the greatest insult in this place. It meant you were at the very bottom of the social pile.

A nothing. A zero. An object of contempt.

I could see I was going to be at home here.

The ball hit my face, my shoulder, my chest, but I didn't flinch. Even when it was thrown purposefully and with full force, I willed my body to stay upright, because my will would be my only defence against the bastards who worked and lived in Winlaton. I didn't join the other girls in the rec room when we went back into section. Mrs Somersett had instructed the staff to put me in isolation in my room. My bed had been removed into the passage and it was just me, the board floor and the brick wall for company. I was to get to know the pattern of those bricks intimately in the weeks and months that followed. I counted those bricks with the same frequency I counted the deductions from my pocket money each week.

Fawdry, nil amount.

I'd been in Goonyah for just over a week when I was called to attend at the doctor's surgery in the administration block. This was part of the induction procedure and no girl could be transferred to another section until she'd had a medical examination, a full gynaecological check for pregnancy and venereal disease. I knew I wasn't pregnant and I knew I didn't have venereal disease, and I definitely knew I wasn't going to allow any doctor to examine me. My aversion to doctors magnified after the other girls told me about the methods he used and the feelings of degradation he elicited through his rough use of the speculum, his unfeeling attitude, and coarse comments.

My refusal to comply was met with the same uninventive punishment, two days locked in my room without my bed. This was taken out into the passage each morning, so I wouldn't be tempted to make myself comfortable, and returned to my room at bedtime. I was the last to get dressed of a morning and the first to get into my nightie and wash my underwear each night. I ate all my meals in my room, and the only time I was allowed out was to use the toilet and dry scrub a section of the long passage, but only ever the section most distant from the rec room and always under supervision. I wasn't permitted to come in contact with anyone except staff, who acted as if I wasn't there. I thought of all the times I'd prayed for invisibility. It had been slow in coming but I had it now, existing on a parallel plane where I could observe life without participation.

The doctor came once a fortnight so I had two weeks reprieve before I had to go through the whole procedure again. I had my period during this time, so there was no need for me to have a pregnancy examination, and the staff certainly knew when any girl had her period. Sanitary pads were kept locked in the store, which could only be accessed by a staff member. Any girl requiring a pad had to ask for one and each subsequent replacement was only provided after showing the soiled pad, and only then if the staff concerned deemed it to be sufficiently full. If successful with an exchange, the used pad was then put into burner on the wall, every action supervised and recorded.

The doctor's visit came around again and I refused to leave the section as before. I was threatened with all sorts of punishment, but I wouldn't budge and back into my room I went. No contact with anyone except staff, who averted their eyes and remained mute when they placed my meals on the floor. I wasn't allowed to listen to the radio. With nothing to distract me I had a lot of time to think back over my life, trying to identify a time I might have changed the course of events, and each time I'd end up at the beginning. It seemed to me the die had been cast at the time of my birth. Having experienced the grief of losing a baby to miscarriage I just could not comprehend how a mother could give away her own child and the questions of *why* and *who* chased themselves around my troubled mind. I now had nothing but contempt for my birth mother, rejecting her as she had discarded me. What kind of woman would leave her child to live this life? It defied explanation in my immature mind, and the questions and thoughts looped and fused until I felt my head would split from the pressure.

Other girls were admitted and transferred from Goonyah to the other sections while I, through my own stubborn determination, remained on security. I was under a lot of pressure to conform. Some staff even took the time to speak with me, as against snapping orders and threats and while this could have been interpreted as them showing a more human side, this was not the case. Their motive had nothing to do with my well-being; it was simply an interest in the smooth running of the institution that relied on a flow of girls through the system. Goonyah only had the capacity to take fifteen girls at a time, although it usually ran with less, to ensure a room was available for a returned absconder or someone from another section who may have broken some rule or another. The message I heard most clearly though, was that I could never move from Goonyah until I'd had the medical.

This also meant I could never hope to be released from Winlaton, because of the progressive system of movement through the sections. Every girl began their stay on Goonyah, and usually worked their way to Warrina within two to four weeks. Transfer from Warrina to Karingal might take three to six months, depending on behaviour, however, some girls were released from Warrina.

I'd been on Goonyah for almost six weeks and, during this time, I'd only been outside the section once, on the day of the netball game. It must have been easier to keep us all cooped up in the small rec, where we could be watched from the comfort of the duty office. I didn't care that much about getting out of Goonyah, in a strange way I felt almost safe there, but I did want to be released from Winlaton so the next time the doctor came I went meekly to my fate. Once outside the security lock area of the porch, I felt the air on my face for the first time in almost six weeks.

It was a sweet moment.

It needed to be.

I went like a lamb to the slaughter, ushered into a room where an elderly doctor, and a crone in a nursing sister's uniform, exorcised their own demons on the unconsenting bodies of young girls.

Clothes off.

Put on the cotton gown.

Get on the table and open your legs.

The sister locked my ankles in the canvas straps of the stirrups attached to each side of the examination bed. White, soft, useless legs, bent at an unnatural angle, with knees that shook. I knew I couldn't walk away from this indignity. My backside lipped over the drop-away end of the bed, suspended in a misery of time.

There are no words to describe the cold shock of the speculum as the doctor rammed it into my exposed vagina and screwed it open, his eyes riveted on my face as he worked. I willed myself away to the secret recess of my mind, away from the pain of prodding spatulate sticks and the weight of his palm as it pushed down on my stomach. I wondered if it was always like this, or if this extreme treatment was an additional punishment for my previous refusals to come into his parlour. I looked down the length of my body to the strands of thin hair stretched across his spotted scalp, his face mere inches from his handiwork. I felt his hot breath on my skin and I recoiled back into myself to a place of disconnected observation.

Once his examination was over, the speculum was unscrewed and removed, and my legs released from their temporary prison. I slipped off the edge of the high bed and the jolt as my feet hit the floor rebounded into my pelvic area. There were no footstools here for bad girls. No assistance and no compassion, but the violation was over and I could look towards working my way out of this place. Oh, human rights, where were you?

A week later, I was transferred to Warrina. Goodbye lock downs and brick walls. Farewell brown passage and the endless dry scrubbing. Goodbye and bad luck Mrs fucking section chief.

Warrina section had been built on the same floor plan as Goonyah, but with the walls plastered and painted. The bedrooms held two beds, each with a candlewick bedspread with more empty spaces than wicking. The floors were covered in the same institutional marbled rubbery floor covering, and a corner wardrobe was provided to hold the possessions we didn't own. Some rooms even had floor rugs. The windows were of a wooden casement style and, while they couldn't be opened wide, there was at least the illusion of letting the outside in, and the view of stars in the night sky was unbroken through the wide pane of glass. All internal doors, except for the store and the duty office, remained unlocked during the day, and I could use the toilet without asking permission. It was a strange freedom after the tight confinement of Goonyah.

All girls on the open sections were expected to be involved in either school or industry during the day. At sixteen, I was considered too old for school, so the choice was limited to the main kitchen, demonstration kitchen or the laundry. Girls on kitchen duty worked different hours to the other industries and seen as an elite group. Their uniform was blue. Demonstration kitchen taught girls the skill of cake decorating. It was supposed to be limited to six weeks per girl, but the group never seemed to change. Everyone wanted to be in demo kitchen. They wore a pink uniform. The laundry girls worked the longest hours and they worked hard under a staff who tried to hide her age under a shock of dyed black hair. The uniform here was green. Nobody wanted to work in the laundry.

I began working in the laundry on my second day on Warrina. The washing machines ran on the almost raw carbolic disinfectant that invaded my eyes and nose and throat, and eroded my soul. Each section had a different linen changing day. Tuesday for Goonyah, Wednesday for Warrina, and Friday for Karingal, and the workload on these three days was relentless. Towels and nightgowns from all the sections were done on Thursdays, and washing for the kitchens was done daily. All washing was collected from the sections each morning and taken to the laundry in canvas trolleys, then washed and dried and returned to the section on the same day. I hadn't liked the ironing room in the convent and I didn't like the laundry here, and I hated the colour green. I wished I could be in demo kitchen, because I thought that I was more of a pink person.

There were many other differences between the sections. Lesbianism, or physical relationships between inmates, was controlled on Goonyah through tight containment and constant supervision. Although there was strict supervision on Warrina, the movement of girls between the section and their daytime activities provided opportunities for closer friendships to develop. The emotional deprivation of the institution, and the need for human contact, often pushed these friendships into more intense physical relationships. The sharing of rooms offered additional settings for shared intimacy, and petty jealousies and lover's tiffs were common.

I shared a room with a generous-sized Greek girl, who wavered between declarations of avowed homosexuality and short periods of heterosexuality. I became her target. It was an odd situation, in which she stalked me with predatory intention throughout the day, and yet left me alone during the long hours of the night when we were locked in the room together. One day she bailed me up in the bathroom area, pushing me into a shower recess, where she attempted to kiss me. I squirmed and twisted and fought the good fight and she gave up when another girl entered the area. On another occasion, when I went into the bedroom during the day to collect something, she pounced on me from the top of the wardrobe and pinned me against my bed. She latched her uninvited mouth onto my neck and gave me a painful love bite. Maybe she thought if she gave me the reputation I might be more open to her advances. Who knows? I didn't waste too much time trying to figure it out though, my sole focus was on my own survival.

I began to look backwards to Goonyah, and wish for the security it afforded from the stress of surviving the perversions of others. When I wasn't busy looking backwards, I looked for a more immediate solution to my problem, the fence. I only mixed with other girls who were serious about absconding and even then I was selective. I had no interest in girls whose interest didn't extend beyond sex and partying. If I was to get out of this place I intended to stay out, and that meant I needed to stay away from the city and inner suburbs and known trouble spots. When I had the opportunity, I studied the fence. I looked for blind spots where it couldn't be seen from the sections and I looked for blind spots in staff vigilance. I also looked for areas of the fence where the coils of barbed wire were less concentrated. And I waited.

Two months passed before I was told to expect visitors one Sunday. Graham and Pauline had been living at Flinders Naval Base and were making the trip out to Nunawading to see me. On visiting day, I dressed neatly in section clothes of skirt, blouse, and cardigan, with black lace up shoes and white socks. Visits began at one o'clock and I waited anxiously. By two o'clock, I thought they'd changed their mind about visiting and, by two thirty, I was sure of it. I knew it had been too good

49

to be true. I looked at my worthless self and accepted no one would or could ever care about me.

I felt a deep sadness, but crying was never going to be an option so I looked for another release for my pain, finding an external replacement for this. I borrowed a sewing needle and a piece of black chalk someone had sneaked into the section and proceeded to brand myself as the undesirable I believed myself to be. I wet the top of the chalk with spittle, covered the needle with the sodden chalk, and pricked myself on the back of my thumb between the first and second knuckle. In and out I worked the needle. Spitting, stirring, and pricking in masochistic frenzy. The blood that ran became the tears I couldn't shed. It mixed with the black and I tattooed it back into my thumb. Every stab was a stab against the disarray and disaster of my life until, from the distance, I heard footsteps approaching the room. I pulled my sleeve over the bloodied thumb.

'Visitors for you, Merlene. You'd better get over to the front now.'

The staff escorted me across to the rear of the administration building and admitted me to the visitor's area. Graham and Pauline could not hide the shock in their eyes when they saw me as they took in the clothes, the lank hair, and my naked face. Graham was angry at the treatment he'd received from the staff, having to show ID and hand in his wallet and Pauline's handbag. He said he wouldn't come back again. We made small talk for a while, but we were all uncomfortable in the unnatural surroundings. I felt they were ashamed of me and disappointed in what they saw. And why not? I was ashamed of myself and my thumb throbbed relentlessly beneath the ribbed band of my cardigan sleeve as a reminder of this.

After the visit, I was strip searched and made to do a number of star jumps while naked. They were so busy looking for contraband they failed to see the raised black welt on my thumb. My hair was thoroughly searched with crooked, poking, fingers, until the staff were satisfied I had nothing secreted there, then I was taken back to my section. It had been another demoralising experience and I'd had enough. I sought freedom with a vengeance. Another girl, Jan, was as eager to get out as I was and we plotted and planned and waited for our chance.

The opportunity presented itself a few days later when Boof and Jan managed to sneak away from the school building. We decided on a spot behind Karingal to scale the fence, where we were unlikely to be disturbed by staff. Boof stood with her back against the fence, hands linked in front of her, as Jan made the first assault on the fence. I watched as she grabbed the bottom of the vee and walked her legs up the corrugations of the fence. She climbed her hands up the metal pole and swung herself up and through the barbed wire.

Then it was my turn. Boof was beginning to weary from her effort and urged me to hurry before she collapsed under my weight. I ran my feet up the wall, amazed at my own lightness and speed. I had difficulty moving through the rows of barbed wire and opted to hoist my leg over the top instead of climbing through the strands. The barbs hooked into my skin and pierced my legs as I straddled the wire, but the rush of adrenalin overtook the pain. I extricated myself, climbed through the coils, and made my way awkwardly over the arm of the vee on the other side. Jan stood on the grass below urging me to hurry in case someone came down the road to Winbirra and caught us.

It was a long way down from the top of the wire to the ground below so I shut my eyes and let go of the pole. But I didn't go anywhere. I hung suspended by my cardigan, which had caught on the extended arm of the vee. The moment seemed to last forever, before I began a slow motion fall as my arms slipped out of the sleeves. I tried to grab at the cardigan as I fell, but it held tight. One shoe fell off in the descent, but there was no time to look for it. We were going to be missed at the next perimeter search when the staff saw my red cardigan waving from the top of the fence.

We took off through the adjacent bush, neither of having any idea where we were or where we were headed. I hobbled on one shoe, and bled from numerous holes in my arms, legs and other parts of my body, but freedom was a heady blend that numbed all else. We eventually came out of the bush near a new housing estate, walking up the suburban footpaths arm in arm, exalting our success. We were discussing how to find our bearings when I heard the sound of a dog barking. Dogs plural, barking. I was familiar with the sound. I'd heard it every night from the dogs that patrolled the compound of a night. I heard the sound of a car engine and remembered it from another night time experience, and the voice I had come to know so well.

'Stop you girls! I've got the dogs!'

Jan and I looked at each other and took off running. We ran across backyards and over fences, terror pumping our legs in our bid to stay ahead of the dogs that bayed and barked above their mistress' voice. I scaled one fence and hooked my backside on a paling, which let me down with a jolt when it snapped in half. We were in a backyard when we heard the dogs getting closer and, fearful of running into a trap, opened a low door in the foundation and entered the crawl space under the house. A small terrier followed us and snarled and yelped as we lay motionless. Movement from the residents inside the house drifted down through the floorboards; a mother's voice etched with concern as she soothed her children, then a sharp knock on the front door followed by the patter of feet and then Mrs Somersett's voice.

'Have you seen two girls? They've escaped from the institution up the road.'

And the women's voice saying no, she hadn't seen anyone. She'd been inside with her children, who could be heard crying in another room.

The terrier snarled at my arm.

'Why is your dog barking? Does he always bark like that...for no reason?'

And the woman kept up her denial, trying to brush off Mrs Somersett, needing to protect her children from the mad girl escapees and the woman with the dogs.

'Could I have a look around the back then...just to make sure? These girls are quite dangerous.'

Mrs Somersett was nothing if not persistent.

'No, I told you it's nothing. Would you leave now please?'

I heard the door close and our pursuer and her dogs got in the jeep and drove away slowly. I lay quite still, too afraid to move in case the terrier bit me. Jan wanted to leave immediately, but I was reluctant. I didn't trust Mrs Somersett. She knew we were in the vicinity and was probably waiting up the road or around a corner somewhere.

'Come on Merlene. We can't afford to wait here. The woman might ring the cops.'

'But what if the dog bites me?'

I could feel the blood seeping from the fence cuts so what did it matter if I got another hole in my body?

Jan was already on the move, shimmying on her stomach across the dusty ground. I stared at the terrier in defiance and made my move, following in Jan's slide. Once we were both outside, we scaled a side fence and ran blindly up the street. We ran until we ran out of houses, and the gutters gave way to dirt floored ditches, then we slowed because we were finally safe.

A car slowed behind us and I turned to see the white divvy van and its uniformed occupants. I ran through the bush in my one shoe and holey sock. I ran with legs caked with blood and dirt. I ran until I came to a wide creek and then I stopped, because there was nowhere to run.

The police drove us back to Winlaton and assisted staff to escort us to Goonyah, where they were greeted by boos and jeers from inmates returning to their sections from the industry block. The metal gate unlocked and we waited for the inner door to open.

Hello again Mrs Section chief. Surprise, surprise you fucken old bitch. I looked up at the clock on the wall of the duty office. I'd had one hour of freedom.

I was back in Goonyah. I'd failed in my bid for freedom. Locked in my room for forty-eight hours with no bed. No radio. No diversions apart from my self-accusatory thoughts. Isolation had a strange effect on me and I found compensation for the sensory deprivation in increased inventiveness. I was my own company. I resumed my old relationship with the red bricks and walked their zigzag path in the freedom of my mind. I was away in a place where hate was the main course and revenge served as dessert. A sweet dessert.

My hearing was attuned for any sound, for footsteps approaching my door or snippets of conversation. I thought if I behaved badly enough I might get to speak with a social worker, or even a psychiatrist. I knew if I could just speak with someone and explain my situation, they'd see I shouldn't be here. Footsteps came closer and I saw an eye, always one eye that looked through the vertical slot in the door. This eye had no lines around it. The skin was smooth but the eye spoke with malice.

'We're gunna get you when you get out.'

I recognised the speaker, a day old chicken in the pecking order. A nobody of no consequence, but I understood the meaning behind her threat. 'Get you' meant rape, and the 'we' meant pack rape. I looked at the eye, smug behind the security of the metal door, and quelled my fear lest my weakness show.

'You'd better make it good then bitch, because you'll only get one shot.'

I heard the staff screech at her from the other end of the passage. That's what happens when you take you eye off the ball, it rolls away from you. The eye bids me goodbye.

'We're gunna get you.'

And I return the farewell. 'Just fuck off, you slimy bitch.'

I realized the population had changed since I left the section two weeks before. There'd been staff changes too. More ten pound Poms from the nearby migrant hostel with their emotional deficits and Borstal mentalities. One of these had been flexing her muscle since my return, always addressing me in a loud and aggressive manner, while looking down the passage for approval from her colleagues. It seemed I'd no sooner settled myself into a position on the floor, leaning against my friend, the wall, than she'd ground her key in the lock and ordered me out to dry scrub the passage.

With so many cuts and tears to my legs and arms, kneeling was extremely painful, and I was unable to exert a lot of pressure on the brush. She stood over me, critical of every stroke I made, proud of the power she could exert. I tried to tune her out, but her voice penetrated my resolve.

'You've missed a bit back there...you'll have to do it over...do it properly or you can keep on scrubbing.'

The long passage was divided into three sections by invisible lines. One section was the usual length anyone had to scrub at one time. It was as much as the knees and back could take in one stint. I came to the end of my part and stood up.

'What do you think you're doing? You'll stop scrubbing when I tell you to stop.'

An echo of my mother's voice joined in.

'Do as you're told. Do as you're told. Don't ask me why. Don't answer back.'

Phewit! Phewit! The pressure cooker steamed and screamed alarm, loosening a rage of expletives.

'You fucken cunt. You fucken miserable bitch. Don't tell me what to fucken do. I scrubbed your fucken passage. Now fuck off and leave me alone.'

Bravery ran from her slack jaw and fear filled her eyes.

'Don't you talk to me like that. Now get down on your knees and scrub.'

'Didn't you hear me you fucken bitch, I said FUCK YOU. FUCK YOU, you fucken low life key carrying bitch.'

55

I threw the brush and it crashed into the metal of the big rec door. The girls locked in the small rec heard the ruckus and responded to it with cat calls and by banging on the door.

'I'll get the chief.'

'Like I fucken care. What'll she do? Lock me in my room?' I laughed at the emptiness of threat.

'Get back in your room now!'

She motioned towards the open door of my room, as other staff came running up the passage, not looking very efficient now. She was looking pretty silly and she knew I could see this. The chief sent her back to the duty office and tried to take control above the sound of screaming and banging coming from the other end of the section. My rage spent for the moment, reduced once more to its simmering point just beneath the surface, I turned and entered my room before I could be ordered to do so. Taking this power left the chief looking confused, but she sought to take control anyway as she locked the door.

'You can stay locked for an extra day for that!'

Thank you again Mrs Fucken Chief. Thank you for giving me an extra twenty-four hours grace before I have to meet my would-be attackers. I arranged my backside on the wooden floors, leant back against the wall, and smiled at the wrinkled eye that watched me through the slot.

All too soon I was released back into the general population of the section and I went with feigned courage and empty bluff. When all the girls were back in the rec room after breakfast and chores completed, I faced them down, speaking to the owner of the eye who'd passed the threat on when I was in solitary.

'I know what you're all up to, so go ahead and do it if you think you're fucken good enough, but one of you must have come up with the idea first, so why don't you have a go on your own?'

They looked at each other with uncertainty, and then looked to their spokesperson for direction. Just as I thought. A little nobody trying to gain a reputation at my expense.

'We've changed our minds. We've decided to do it to someone else now.'

I kept my back to the wall, anyway. There's no point in taking chances in this shaky world.

Jan had been released back into the section before me, because I'd been treated to an extra day in isolation, and we stuck together most of the time when she wasn't in school. I relied on her to bring me news of the world outside of Goonyah, the small world of the wider institution. Time hung heavily and every day took an eternity to pass. Confined in the small rec were some of the most damaged girls in the state; the abused and the neglected, those on offence charges, and those whose very existence appeared to be an offence; those who saw sex as a survival skill and worked it, the pregnant, the mentally ill, the submissive, the sad and the sorry. Many broke under the strain of confinement and the uncertainty as to when and where their future lay, or even if they had a future. There were many girls who, like me, were given no indication as to when they might be released and it robbed us of all sense of hope.

Any sharp object smuggled in to the section became a tool for self-mutilation, as girls slashed their arms and legs hoping they'd be re-classified to Larundel, a psychiatric facility. Occasionally this worked and I watched as bloodied girls were carted off, never to return. A pregnant girl bashed her head repeatedly against a brick wall to change the focus of her pain. Another punched herself repeatedly in her swollen stomach, seeking to kill her unwanted child, while the staff sat with their backs turned sipping their morning tea.

Many times I despaired of surviving this place and I fanned the flames of my rage to keep depression at bay. Like a person lost in the snow, I had to stay awake to remain alive; to be vigilant and focus solely on keeping my anger active. Any time I felt myself slipping into the self-pity that heralds melancholia, I only had to look at the Terylene dresses gathered in the duty office. Vicious Pommy bitches, whose lack of intelligence and human understanding kept the place on the edge of anarchy. They were forever on the lookout for any breach of rules, no matter how small, to bring diversion to their own day.

Christian ethics were adhered to in principle only. Every meal began with the saying of grace when we'd stand behind our chairs and thank the Lord for what we were about to receive. I made this one of my silent protests, for what did I have to be thankful for? It was a win only I knew about. I kept my face turned away and my mouth firmly closed and it felt good. Then someone changed my seating position and I was face to face with the staff on duty in the corner. I looked at the ceiling as grace was recited, my mouth closed against the hypocrisy of it, taking my seat with the others when it was over.

'You there. What do you think you're doing?' It's funny how I always knew the 'you' referred to was me, but I ignored it anyway.

'Stand up when I'm speaking to you.' It was the new staff again. A slow learner. 'Stand up and say grace!'

She was leaning over me now. A giantess in Terylene stripes, 'STAND UP!'

She liked an audience this one, and her voice again attracted the attention of staff in the duty office. I heard the clank of keys as the door was opened from the other side. I told her to back off, to move away and give me room to stand, pushing my chair back hard against her legs to make my point. She moved then all right. I felt myself coming alive as the anger surged and erupted.

'FUCK YOU! Why can't you leave me alone? I haven't done anything wrong!'

'You have to say grace.'

Say grace? Thank God or Jesus, or whoever was responsible for this degradation. I didn't think so.

I was removed from the dining room to scrub the passage. I refused to do this and I watched my bed leave my room, in its regular migration into the passage. I painted the section in the vibrant language of the streets as I was assisted to my room.

'Only one fucken day, Chief? What a fucken shame.'

'Two days for that, Merlene!'

'Thank you, Chief.'

My meal was brought to my room and placed just inside the door. Don't get too close now. You never know what I might do. Mrs New Staff looked smug. She'd been vindicated. I never ate that meal, nor did I eat for the whole of the next day. They didn't like this. I smiled at their consternation. I'd found another way to empower myself. Silence and hunger were a powerful combination.

Mrs Somersett was usually called to the section after incidents of this nature, so we saw each other frequently. We shared a mutual hate relationship. She often had the gate man with her for an extra show of strength. Other girls had told of being bashed by him, but I hadn't had the pleasure so far. I guess she could deal with a girl of my size on her own. The gate-man was a well-built man and very tall, with hands the size of dinner plates. I'd seen him hit other girls, and one hit knocked them off their feet.

So the day of the grace thing I sat and waited for the sound of her arrival. I could always tell when it was her. She had a unique way of clanking the keys and throwing back the door as she entered the section so it banged against the adjoining wall. I could hear the fury in her walk as she strode towards my room, but on this day the keys had a muted sound, and the tread up the passage was softer and less anger driven.

I dared to hope it was a psychiatrist or social worker coming to see me at last.

The door opened and I saw Miss Doran, the Director of Winlaton, standing in the passage. This kind and gentle woman had the capacity to do what those who tried to contain and tame me could never achieve, and I felt hot tears threaten to melt the ice in my eyes. I caught them before my weakness showed and we looked at each other through shining eyes. Miss Doran talked to me as if I was a person. She listened to me as I spoke. I didn't have to swear or raise my voice. I told her about the amount of time I was forced to spend in my room, the excessive punishments for minor infringements and the provocation from staff. She checked my wounds and I felt the healing in her touch.

I heard her speak with the staff after she left the room, because she left my door open, instructing them not to lock me in. They were to put my bed back in immediately and allow me to return to the rec room in another hour. I watched the sour faces as they carried my bed in. I didn't smirk. I didn't gloat in any way. I only said four words.

'Thank you very much.'

And then I smiled and stayed sitting on the floor.

News of Miss Doran's intervention went around the institution staff like wildfire. My popularity with the other inmates rose dramatically, while the staff would hardly give me the time of day, but I had bigger things to worry about. The doctor was due for his fortnightly rounds. There was no way I was going to have another medical. I'd only been out of the institution for an hour and I'd been running for most of that time. The only males I'd encountered had been the police officers so, if I had to have an examination to rule out pregnancy or VD, what did that say about the police?

Mrs Somersett continued with her own brand of provocation. Someone arranged for films to be shown on the section and the big rec was set up for the evening. It turned out the films were travelogues on Tasmania and I was looking forward to seeing familiar scenery. There were three of us on section with ties to Tasmania, two girls from Hobart and me. After the kitchen girls had finished the dishes that night, Mrs Somersett came into the rec room to tell us what was expected of us in relation to our behaviour, and then she took me out into the passage. I was told I wouldn't be seeing the films, because my behaviour didn't deserve any privileges. I was to be locked in my room for the evening. Leading me up the passage, past a bed resting against the wall, she locked me in the room closest to the big rec, warning me that if I acted out in any way, the rest of the section wouldn't be allowed to see the films. Peer pressure was often used as a control device, so I was well aware she'd follow through with this if I made any protest at all. She then took the other two Tasmanian girls, locking one in the room across the passage from me, and the other in the room next to mine. I couldn't think why she'd placed us in rooms other than our own, until I heard the sound for the films begin; a cinema type roar of sound that always heralded any film or movie news, before melting into distinguishable dialogue. Then I understood. She wanted us to hear what we were missing out on and I wondered what unhappiness drove such mental cruelty. I put my hands over my ears and took myself to a place in my mind where no-one could reach me.

I was subdued the following day as I tried to process what had happened the night before, and contemplating the doctor's pending visit and how I was going to get out of it. Mrs New Staff was on duty and that was always a problem for me, because I never knew which direction she'd attack from next. I hated it when she was on dining room duty, because of the officious manner in which she attempted to carry out her duties. She always found fault at line up. Whether it was the fold of someone's socks, or because she felt their arm wasn't held out straight enough, and this day was no different. I could feel my anger rise as she started on me.

'Fold those socks down properly...pull those sleeves down...get that arm out straight!'

I did as she said, but my stomach knotted with suppressed resentment and anxiety. I felt this wasn't going to be a good day and when I looked at the table I knew it for sure.

It was the egg that did it. A simple boiled egg. I'd only ever tried to eat one since I'd been here, but I just couldn't manage to swallow the rubbery contents of an egg that had been boiled to buggery and back. I averted my face while grace was said and, as I sat down, I pushed the egg towards the middle of the table, saying to the girl next to me.

'I'm not eating that.' It was common practice to offer up any food you didn't want to anyone else who might want it. It happened at every meal and it was no big deal, or it shouldn't have been.

'Don't let me hear you swear again.'

How did I know she was talking to me? Was it pure instinct, or simply an understanding of her inability to broaden her focus? I opted for ignoring her.

'I SAID, don't swear! Now STAND up.'

I tried to tell her I hadn't sworn, and the other girls at my table attested to this, but she insisted I had. She wanted me to stand up and apologise to her, but I knew it was more than that. It was about the power she gained through her complete domination over me, so I obliged. I jumped out of my seat and shouted as I walked towards her, 'I didn't fucken swear, you deaf bitch, but if you're going to fucken accuse me of something I haven't done, then I'll give you something to accuse me of.'

I launched into a tirade of expletives as foul as it was inventive. I called her every name that came to mind, with every insulting adjective I could think of. I was aware other staff had entered the room. I saw their lips moving in speech, but their words were lost in my search for justice. And then I was done. It was almost a competition to see who would break the silence first, but my opponent broke the stand-off and ordered me to my room.

'You only have to stay there until you cool down, then you can come out again.'

This woman had no idea. She offered to leave my bed in if I promised not to sit on it. It seemed obvious Miss Doran had given her some instructions on humane containment, but I didn't grace her offer with a response. Was I supposed to be grateful for a situation she had initiated?

I'd no sooner settled in my room than she was back with my meal. Maybe someone had read her the regulations relating to food deprivation as well. I acknowledged her gesture.

'You can take that and stick it up right up your fucken arse, you bitch.'

Sometime later she returned to let me out. All I had to do scrub a section of passage and I could go back into the small rec. I started to argue that I'd already been punished by being placed in my room, and for something I hadn't done in the first place, but I could see her trigger finger on the keys. I took the brush and tried to scrub my anger away. I visualised her face on the floor, seeking to erase it under the stiff bristles, but it only sharpened my hatred of her. I'd done the usual one third of the passage when she said I could stop.

'Come down here and apologise and you can go back in the rec.'

Apologise? No way would I apologise to this bitch. I didn't care what she did to me I would never apologise to her.

'Get fucked!' She flinched as I walked towards her, one eye on her companions in the duty office, 'you're the greatest fucken bitch I've ever met - and that's saying something in this place.'

She sent me back to scrub another third of the passage and, when I still refused to apologise, she told me to scrub the rest, and all of this I did. I would have scrubbed my way to hell and back before I apologised to her. Once I'd completed the task, I began to walk back up the passage away from her.

'Where do you think you're going? Just bring the brush back here and I'll let you in the rec room.'

Yeah, sure you will. After I grovel and lick your boots. I ignored her continued orders and kept walking until I was at the other end of the passage. She was still bleating about bringing the brush back when I took off at a run, my arm rotating in best Bradman fashion, before I made the bowl of the century.

'Here's your fucken brush then bitch.'

The brush torpedoed towards her and she just made it inside the duty office before it crashed against the door. This lit the fuse in the rec room and the section erupted in howls of sympathetic energy from the other inmates. I ran into the shower area, a door-less alcove with open cubicles and exposed plumbing, where I wedged myself in and around the hand basin pipes and waited for the posse to arrive.

The siege was long and the negotiations stalled before they began. I wanted the slate wiped clean, as the initial action had been initiated by the staff. I didn't want to have to apologise or demean myself in any way. They wanted me to go into time-out and to apologise to the staff I'd sworn at. The section was at boiling point. A number of girls had been locked in their rooms for using threatening language to staff and there was a real danger of a riot occurring. Any perceived injustice against an inmate could unite the spot fires that smouldered continuously. The place was a tinderbox, and already girls from other sections were screaming words of support from beyond Goonyah's exclusion zone. I was a spark to be extinguished.

I wasn't enjoying any of this. It had taken on a surreal tone, where I was more of a spectator than participator. This wild-eyed, foul-mouthed, girl whose scarred limbs wound so inelegantly around the pipes, was a stranger to me. I had no more control over her behaviour, than those endowed with responsibility for the security and well-being of the section population. The attending staff numbers increased and the gate-man was eventually called to flex his muscles, but I remained fixed in position. My legs cramped and the pain penetrated my trance-like state, but I didn't know how to stop the roller coaster of defiance. Then I heard familiar footsteps as Miss Doran entered the section. There was something about this woman that always had the potential to intercept my anger and begin the thaw of my iced-over emotions. She was a true humanitarian, at a time in Australian children's welfare history, when punitive consequence was the prescribed formula for anyone breaking the rules.

The staff were ordered back to the staff room and Miss Doran spoke to me as a person of value. I responded accordingly, my words forced into a higher pitch as they detoured around the lump in my throat. She assisted me to unwind my legs from the pipes, and massaged feeling back into them when they threatened to buckle beneath me. Miss Doran could have sent me into the fires of hell and I would have gone willingly. But she only sent me to my room, with bed remaining and door open, until I and the section had settled. I complied willingly. She talked with me about my future within and beyond Winlaton and told me she'd speak with me again in two weeks' time when she returned from holidays. I never got locked in my room for a long time after that day, although they found other ways to bend Miss Doran's directive.

I did, however, spend many hours dry scrubbing the passage, and when they thought they'd broken me to that task they came up with another. I was no longer just another inmate lost in the system, it felt like I was the only inmate, as the staff continuously looked for evidence of my oppositional defiance. They scrutinized the speed in which I followed an order, the way I wore my clothes, my everyday speech and gestures, and they found fault in every small action.

When I refused to see the doctor the next time he came, I was taken to the big rec, the room furthest away from where the other girls spent their daytime hours. It was July and the middle of a freezing Melbourne winter when the door locked behind me. A row of the same square grilled windows faced out onto the end of the Warrina building and an area between the two buildings that was out of bounds. The only floor covering was a small coir mat that prickled my bare legs, and my only point of diversion was a metal bucket that lay on its side some distance away, where it had bounced off the door when I'd thrown it on protest, nearby was a large wad of wire wool.

The bucket was coated in the scum of use and my task was to scrub it clean, to bring the shine back to its befouled surface. It was one of a number of such items sent over from Pentridge men's prison in Coburg, its rejuvenation to be used as a punishment tool for intractable young girls. I could only guess as to its previous use, but I suspected it had been used as a latrine bucket. It was foul and I refused to touch it. It lay there in its own rejection. Two rejects sharing a room. The only breaks came via my staff-delivered meals, which I ate in an effort to warm my insides. The only conversation was an order to scrub the bucket, spoken as if this was a perfectly ordinary request. Now and again I heard sounds of a scuffle in the passage, and the resonance of raised voices, followed by the unmistakable sound of rubber soles hitting the passage floor in running steps

'Don't scrub the bucket, Merlene,' a voice would call towards my prison and echo in my mind, before the supporter was caught and returned to the other end of the section. I didn't care that much about what other people thought. I knew I was on my own.

That night I was given my nightie to change into, although, had I known the repercussions of this, I would have refused to get changed. My clothes were not returned to me the next morning, and I spent the remainder of my time in the big rec dressed only in the thin nightie. It was so cold during the night I lay under the coir mat in an effort to get some warmth into my body. My back ached, and I had to change my position regularly to ease the pressure points where my knees, hips and elbows came in contact with the hard wooden floor. My mind walked the great expanse of the brick wall, and hop scotched across the shadows thrown by the windows, but the biting cold drew me back before I could disappear completely.

When it got too much I got up and walked around, feet frozen against the floor, rubbing my limbs to generate heat. The hour before dawn was the coldest. White frost coated the inside of the windows, and I huddled with my knees drawn up inside my nightie, where my legs could draw some warmth from my belly. I looked forward to having a warm shower but, when the staff saw I still hadn't touched the bucket, I was told I couldn't have a shower or change my clothes until it was done. I was, however, allowed to have breakfast and I warmed my hands on the outside of the hard plastic cup as I sipped the welcome tea. What the staff saw when they looked through the slot, was a regular lady of the world basking in the sun that followed the heavy frost as I nibbled my toast.

I was worried what they might withhold from me next, concerned they might refuse to let me out to use the toilet, although the solution to that lay in the very cause of my problem, the bucket. The day progressed similar to the one before it. Girls would break away from staff when being escorted to the toilet, to yell some revolutionary message of unity through the closed door. With this extra activity in the section one of the officers must have accidentally flicked the lever to the big rec speaker, and I heard a news report a girl in Tasmania had shot her father. I knew intuitively it was Jill, but I had no way of verifying this as staff were quick to turn it off once they realized their error. This sobering news took my attention away from my own situation as I contemplated the fear that would drive such an action.

A girl from another section risked punishment by entering the exclusion zone, to poke half a White Knight candy bar through the window. I found it when I was returned from a trip to the toilet and I was touched by the gesture. I decided to save the candy for later, which was a fortunate move, because Mrs Somersett ordered staff to withhold all of my meals until I'd complied and given them a shiny bucket. I savoured the sweet and made it last by rationing it out. I'd have one suck and then re-wrap it and hold the taste in my mouth until the memory of it had gone, then I'd repeat the process. This helped me through the first part of the long and painful night, curled in misery under the coir mat. I needed to go to the toilet, but I knew no-one would respond if I banged on the door. There was only one night staff per section, and they spent most of their shift congregated in the relative comfort of the Karingal duty office. I put my arm between my legs and pressed hard, as if to force the urine back into my full bladder. I thought about using the bucket, but I couldn't bring myself to touch it in any way.

I was almost grateful to the staff who escorted me to the toilet in the morning. I felt as if she looked on me with some feeling. Something in her voice tone separated her from the mob, but when she asked me to scrub the bucket I passed off her kind demeanour as just another ruse. Breakfast time passed without any offering, but it didn't worry me too much. I found it easier not to think beyond the moment and then, just before lunch, they were back with another lever.

Nobody on the section was allowed to eat until I'd scrubbed the bucket.

I knew how important mealtimes were in the institution, and more so on Goonyah where there were no other activities to break up the day, although it wasn't so much the food that interested any of us. It was more the opportunity to move beyond the confines of the small room, and a recognisable time division in the day. I was encouraged by support shown throughout the morning as the breakaways called their message through to me.

'Don't scrub the fucken bucket.'

Lunchtime came and went without the usual clatter of the hot box on its journey from the main kitchen. I wondered if the pregnant girls were allowed to eat, or if they were suffering the same deprivation. The afternoon wore on although, without any activity to demarcate the day, it became a blurring of time. The messages of support continued to float up the passage, and sometimes the more fleet of foot would actually make it to my door, but as the sky began to darken, so did the mood of the section.

'You'd better scrub that bucket, we're fucken hungry.'

And after a while it began to get ugly.

'Scrub the fucken bucket or you're dead.'

I didn't blame them for the change in attitude. This was an institution and solidarity had never been a strong point with the inmates. They were right. Why should other people have to suffer for my wrong doing? I looked at the bucket and knew I was beaten. I sat with the thing between my legs and began to scrub. The outer scum from the bucket grasped my fingers, and buried itself in the folds of my nightie, while small fibres of wire broke free from the wadding and stuck into my fingers. I scrubbed backwards and forwards on the same section until I saw the gleam of clean metal, and then I moved to another spot and began again, working my way around the top rim of the bucket. Tears of hopelessness and despair fell and blended with the physical evidence of another person's misery I was attempting to erase. The door opened and footsteps drew closer. I kept my head down and scrubbed.

'Don't scrub anymore, Merlene...you've done enough.'

Done enough? I'd hardly even begun. I looked towards the speaker, and when our eyes met I saw my own defeated spirit reflected in her brimming eyes. It was the same staff who'd taken me to the toilet that morning. Her voice was gentle as she told me again to stop scrubbing, and with this act she caught my spirit before it left me completely.

Miss Doran returned from her holiday and talked with me as she'd promised. She tried to get me to talk about what I wanted to do with my life, but the concept of having the liberty to make my own decisions and control my own destiny was so foreign to me I couldn't respond. In some abstract way, I still thought I'd marry Michael, if I ever got out of Winlaton that was, but I had no real ambition other than to marry and have babies. She expressed concern at the extremity of my behaviour, and decided my inability to conform was due to my overactive mind.

'I think you're too intelligent to just sit around all day, you've got too much time to think.'

I'd never heard anyone suggest I was intelligent before. Not me.

'How would you like to go to our school here? It would give you something to occupy your mind with.'

I thought about Jan and the other girls who went off to school from Goonyah, and how they seemed to be happy to line up to be escorted to the school building. I thought about the colour purple of their uniforms and their interaction with girls from other sections. I thought about being in the open air each day as I walked between buildings.

'Yes, I'd like to go to school.'

The following Monday I lined up with the other girls and waited for staff to escort us to school, eager to leave the section. My purple uniform fitted comfortably and I felt almost normal as I walked slowly around the oval towards the school building. All lessons were undertaken by correspondence under the guidance of a trained teacher. The work was easy, but self-discipline took a greater effort. The teacher had a problem with alcohol and, as the day wore on, she was absent from the room for longer periods of time. Girls who couldn't progress with their lesson without having their work checked, or who needed advice on how to solve a problem, became restless in their boredom. A lack of supervision and direction led to the contagion of aberrant behaviour, and it took all of my resolve to isolate myself from classroom-based deviancy.

The idle periods were taken up with discussion on everybody's favourite subject. Freedom. We talked about what it meant to each person and how best to attain it. This led to discussion on absconding, and it had an unsettling effect on me. I began to look toward the fence and the possibility of escape. I conspired with Jan to abscond again and we considered how to stay out once we had our freedom. We shared the same desire to return to our respective home towns, to return to a place of belonging. I would somehow get to Tasmania and she'd get to Shepparton. We both knew we'd been unwise the last time, to just take off without having a clear plan of how to leave the area, so we decided to stay alert for sounds of traffic or trains from beyond the walls, to give us some indication of highways or rail tracks to follow.

I kept a low profile in the section and Miss Doran had no reason to visit me again. Each night I trained my ears to follow the sound of the trains that passed close by, heading west towards the city of Melbourne. In class, we observed the pattern of the teacher's absences from the room, until we'd identified the optimum time to leave. The day finally came when all the signs were right. Boof came out of the school with us to help us on our way.

A False Freedom

Jan and I went over the fence and hit the ground running. I sustained some deep wounds to my legs from the barbed wire, but there was no time to stop and assess the damage. There was no elation at our freedom. We knew from last absconding experience that any celebration could be premature and of short duration. Our priority was to get out of the area as quickly as possible. It was unlikely we'd be missed for at least an hour, and we wanted to be well gone before then. Our idea had been to find the railway line and follow it to the next station and then jump the train to the city. As long as we left the train before it reached Flinders Street Station, we could probably get through one of the many unattended ticket gates undetected. If that failed, we'd planned to leap from the train as it slowed to a stop coming in to the station, and run across the tracks. But this was a contingency plan only, as my legs had been hobbled by new wounds added to those of my previous effort.

We walked at a steady pace. It wouldn't do to look as if we were running from someone, or something, or some place. I kept my ears tuned for the sound of a train whistle, but the sights and sounds of the outside world intruded; the blend of car, bus and truck engines distorted my sense of direction and Jan was no help either. She'd originally come from rural Victoria, and her lack of experience of city life and sounds disorientated her completely.

I tried to block out the invasion of sound, to recall the train noises that had teased me with their nearness from my position behind the fence. I was sure we were headed in the right direction, and the long blast of a train whistle and the screech of brakes as it entered Nunawading station gave us hope. It was too close to risk getting on the train here, but it gave us a clear direction to the next train stop down the line. All we had to do was follow the rails and, if we still felt wary of discovery, we could keep following the line all the way into Melbourne if need be. We had all the time in the world.

With our matching purple school uniforms, white socks and sandshoes, we passed as ordinary school girls; as long as I kept my cardigan sleeves pulled down to cover the tattoos I'd been adding to since the first one. I noticed one across the top of my knee had almost disappeared, ripped open by the barbed wire, but it wasn't bleeding as heavily as the surrounding cuts. Once again, Jan had hardly any injuries at all, maybe she had thicker skin than mine.

We followed the train line until we came to the car park of a small suburban station. It was here our nerve began to fail for the first time, as we wondered if the police had alerted railway station masters along the line, or whether a ticket inspector might be on the same train. Apprehension by either meant a certain return to the institution. We looked around the almost empty car park, and my wish for divine guidance came in the form newspaper delivery man who watched us with curiosity from his van.

'Are you girls alright?'

Jan and I looked at each other, tongue tied. I said yes, she said no, and we looked at each other for clarity.

'Are you okay?' He asked again, as he looked more closely at our dishevelled appearance.

Jan and I concurred this time with a vocal sound that meant yes, no, and everything in between, a sort of long drawn out 'mmnnnerr'. I could see he was becoming suspicious, so I answered more coherently this time.

'No, we're in trouble. We wagged school and went with these boys and they attacked us. We escaped, but had to leave our school bags behind and now we haven't got our train fare home.'

He looked interested, indignant and puffed with male outrage.

'You need to go to the police and report it.'

'No, we can't do that, if our parents find out they'll kill us,' I'd been fishing before and I knew the feel of one on the hook, 'could you lend us the train fare please?'

He looked at me steadily. Telling lies was hard work, but Jan joined in to help me out.

'We're scared the boys might find us again if we don't get on the train soon.'

He pulled out some change from somewhere between the seats.

'Here, take this, and make sure that you go straight home.'

We took the six shillings of his generosity, thanking him demurely as we promised to go straight home, and we would have gone home if we'd had the means to do so.

It turned out we didn't have to buy a ticket after all, because there wasn't anyone in the ticket box to sell us one. This often happened between peak travel periods with smaller stations. If a ticket inspector got on he'd probably understand, but our luck continued, and no inspector meant we still had six shillings at the end of our journey.

We needed to change from our Winlaton clothes as soon as possible, knowing the police would have a description of them, so we headed for the St Kilda/Middle Park area. I thought some expatriate Tasmanians might still be living in that part and, from there, I hoped to track down my clothes. It didn't happen. I knocked on every door that looked familiar and even some that didn't, but there was no trace of my friends or my clothes.

Jan wanted to head north towards her home in Shepparton, although neither of us had any idea which direction to follow, but I still wanted to find a change of clothes. We walked the long kilometres to Elsternwick, where I hoped to find some residue of past loyalties, but I was in a world apart from my old friends now. Their life had structure and purpose that came from the security of a roof over their head, while my existence was one of uncertainty and need and impermanence, and all wanted to distance themselves in case they were drawn in and down. Even the boys at sixty-six Regent Street, once such close supportive friends, had now grown two years older and wiser. They were wary of trouble in the form of an escapee in need of medical attention.

We hung around for an hour or so, unwanted, and not particularly optimistic of receiving help in any form. We were, quite simply, unsure of where to go next. My knee was swollen and throbbed painfully, an ugly sight of exposed flesh where the clean edges of the lacerations and the larger, open wounds were beginning to merge. The boys from sixty-six said we could stay at their house for the night, but only for one night, and we had to promise to leave first thing in the morning. It gave us a brief respite from the streets while we considered what to do next. A couple of residents from Regent House brought us some food they'd managed to sneak out and we ate this greedily with no thought of where our next meal might come from. They also offered to get some clothes together for us and arranged to meet us the following night at Balaclava Station, several kilometres away from possible apprehension for any of us. Our position, and indeed ourselves, was not something they wanted to associate with.

The following day we took to the streets again and headed towards St Kilda. Because of the frequent police patrols, this was the most dangerous place for us to be, but I thought we could probably blend in with other outcasts and society rejects, and there was something else in the back of my mind. I knew we'd never get anywhere without money. We needed a place to stay and food, and both cost money. We needed to get a job to earn money to support ourselves, but it was a catch 22 situation. We couldn't get a job without a fixed address and presentable clothes to wear. I could see this cycle of unmet need would keep us bound to homelessness and the despair of the fugitive state, unless we found a way to make money, quick money. I watched the working girls as they walked the beat, and the slow pace of the gutter crawlers as they trawled Fitzroy and Acland Streets in search of cheap sex, their intention open and business like.

'Hey girls, are you working?'

I'd learnt the meaning behind this question from my time in the area before my placement in Winlaton. It was the terminology used to ask if a girl was available for prostitution. I answered without looking at the enquirer

'No, we're not.'

They persisted for a while, following us as we tossed our heads in indignation, becoming abusive when we continued with our rejection. Hungry for sex, they'd gun their motors and hunt the block looking for the next likely target. There was no shortage of possibilities down here.

'Maybe one of us will have to prostitute.' I said aloud what had been on my mind although, when I said one of us, I knew I meant Jan. There was no way I'd be able to do it. My strict Methodist upbringing and natural inhibitions would never allow me it.

'It would only take a couple of times, and then we'd have enough to find somewhere to stay, or even to leave the city and go to Shep.'

I threw the last in as a sweetener, after all, there had to be something in it for her. We continue to discuss it in an abstract way over the next few hours. Neither of us felt we'd be able do it, but we were quite willing to pimp for the other. I used my injuries as a reason for abstinence, while Jan cited her tender years, and we were both creative in our excuses. It was going nowhere and neither were we. We'd rejected numerous opportunities from the passing cars and I knew something would have to give soon. I looked at her teenage voluptuousness and back to my lean frame.

'It'll have to be you Jan, because you've got a big bust, and that's what they like.'

I looked at her slyly and I could see she was considering my words.

'You're so much more attractive than I am, and you'd make more money.' She began to look interested. 'I wouldn't tell anybody. I promise.'

I was still waiting for an answer when the flash of a police car U turning in Fitzroy Street caught my eye.

'Jesus, Jan, it's the cops. Run.'

But she was already ahead of me, sprinting up Acland before my words were out. I ran and hobbled and ran again, pushing past the pain, as the need for flight blocked all other sensations. Jan paused for me to catch up, then took off again, until we ran into the side of a utility barring our way in a cross street. The driver threw open the passenger door and told us to get in.

'Go! Go! Jesus, Jan, get down before they see you.'

I spotted the police car as it travelled slowly up the street, while our rescuer took off in the opposite direction and kept on going. He asked us questions and appeared to be interested in, and sympathetic to, our situation. He eventually pulled up in an area where deserted sand dunes protected the highway from Port Phillip Bay, and we talked some more. We told him our story and the plan to meet the Regent House girls at Balaclava Station that night to get some clothes. I told him I just wanted to get back to Tasmania and Jan told him she wanted to get back to Shepparton. We were two kids who thought we knew it all, but we were both way out of our depth.

I was never sure at what point rescuer became predator, or whether this had been his motive all along. The change was subtle. He began initially to suggest we owed him and proposed that sex would be an acceptable method of payment. When we declined, both singularly and together, he offered a monetary incentive. The amount grew with each new request, until he offered his whole pay packet, but neither of us was tempted. He'd already shown he couldn't be trusted and, while he was freely waving his cash around, I knew he had no intention of parting with any of it. He was not a man of honour. Finally, tired of the stand-off, he issued an ultimatum.

'Either one of you do it, and I don't care which one it is, or you can both get out and walk. Now what's it going to be?'

I was concerned at the passing of time. The last rays of the winter sun weakened as dusk moved in from across the bay. I knew we were a long way from Balaclava and concerned we'd never get there in time to meet the girls.

'Please, can't you just take us back?'

'Give it to me, and then I'll take you back, or you can get out.' I could tell he meant business. He was angry now and his voice sounded menacing in the gloom.

'Well, we'll just have to walk then. Come on, Jan.'

We got out of the car and began to walk up the sandy path to the highway beyond, his curses adding urgency to our steps. I heard the motor rev, a threatening rumble behind the warning of his headlights and turned back to see the car bearing down on us, gathering speed as the tyres found traction beneath the surface sand. On one side of the track the dark waters of the bay circled the shore, while on the other side a grassed bank rose steeply to the highway above. There was nowhere to run. The motor roared as it approached, faster now. I grabbed Jan's hand and pulled her towards the bank.

'Come on, just climb. He's going to kill us if we don't.'

We slid, clawed and crawled our way up the unforgiving slope and out of immediate danger, as he stopped the car at the foot of the bank and screamed further threats. Reaching the top, we hid in a stand of cypress and watched him cruise up and down the highway, not willing to let his prey escape so easily. Eventually we watched his tail lights as they disappeared towards Melbourne. Too afraid to try to get a lift from anyone else, we began the long walk to Balaclava. The pain had almost disappeared from my knee now, settling into a dull numbness that allowed me to walk with some speed, but it was all to no avail. As we approached Balaclava Station we saw that the place was alive with police activity.

We'd been betrayed. I couldn't decide whether it had been our recent friend who'd tipped the police off, or whether it had been the girls from Regent House, wanting to remove any threat to their own security. It didn't really matter. It just proved it didn't do to trust anyone and it was another lesson learnt.

We faced our second night of freedom, cold, hungry, and with nowhere to sleep, and we determined to leave Melbourne as soon as possible. In the meantime, we had to find somewhere to get off the streets until morning. An unlocked car offered cramped shelter for the night, and a place to hide from the police whom we were certain had begun a large scale hunt for us by now. I catnapped throughout the night, chilled, uncomfortable and fearful of discovery, and I welcomed the first light of day that was our signal to move on. We joined other homeless people as they emerged from their night shelters, gathering at a nearby toilet block to wash under the freezing water of a solitary cold water tap. A breeze came in from the bay with an iciness that bit deep into my injured leg, sending a misery throughout my whole body, and I found it difficult to look beyond the despair of our situation. I hoped today would be the day Jan would turn a trick and bring in some money. I couldn't be expected to do anything much with my bad leg, and it wouldn't attract too many customers. We spoke of *it* in general terms as we sought shelter amongst the bare trees of winter. The treed gardens of the St Kilda held out skeletal limbs, grey and mottled, a warning to keep moving, and we gravitated once more to Fitzroy Street. This street was pivotal to all activity in the area. It spelt life for those dead to society; a street that never slept.

Another two weeks would pass before we found the correct highway out of Melbourne and a truck driver willing to pick up two unkempt girls in the hope of a sexual exchange. Two weeks that became a blur of false leads, starts and false hope in every direction. Most nights we spent in the cramped confines of parked cars, cold and uncomfortable; tired, sore and sorry for ourselves. Many nights we ceased speaking to each other at all, fed up with our own miserable company, and bristling from some real or imagined slight. Other days the sun shone more brightly and it was possible to see better times ahead.

On one such day we'd jumped the train to Caulfield, where I'd hoped to catch up with some old work mates, but news of our need had preceded our arrival and we were met with the blank faces and averted eyes of the unwilling. Walking back to the station we passed a shoe shop that Jan had looked in on our way past earlier, spotting a pair of boots she liked. She didn't have a problem with stealing. She excelled at it, but it made me anxious. I was still hopeless as a lookout too, as *thou shalt not steal* planted a guilty look on my face.

She stopped at the shoe shop and cautioned me to wait while she went inside. I knew what she intended to do, but I could also see the risks involved.

'Don't Jan, it's not worth getting caught for a lousy pair of boots.'

I was still nagging at her to give it a miss when she turned and walked in the door. I was certain she'd get caught and, angry she'd placed us in this position, walked quickly down the street. I wanted to put some distance between us.

I didn't turn when I heard the footsteps behind me, walking faster as I waited for the hand of apprehension to grab me on the shoulder. But the walker caught up with me and passed without missing a step, the quickly spoken words the only sign of recognition.

'Keep walking. Quick. I think they saw me.'

I looked at the back of this stupid girl and my anger rose again. 'Bloody hell, Jan! I told you not to take anything. Just piss off away from me.'

'Just keep walking,' she parroted.

She ignored my words and I slowed my steps to watch her retreating back, and then I saw them; the object of her haste and my anger. On her feet she wore the most hideous pair of fake leopard skin slipper boots, which flopped at a crazy angle as she walked. I began to laugh and I ran my hobbled gait to catch up with her, but she increased her pace, still bristling from my earlier comments. In the end I had to stop. I'd developed the stitch in my side from the combination of trying to run while overcome with laughter. Jan turned to face me and I laughed louder, doubled over at the sight before me.

'Your feet,' I spluttered between laughs, 'look at your bloody feet. Oh my God, your feet. '

'What? What's so funny?' She looked down at her feet and back to me again, 'what?'

'You stupid bloody idiot, and I suppose you left your other shoes in the shop.'

'So?'

'So you've traded your old shoes for two left slippers. Have a good look at your feet.'

It was too much and my laughter now bordered on hysteria. The look on her face as she realized what she'd done set me laughing again, and this time she joined in with me. Jan may have been slow on the uptake, and not the best shoe thief in the world, but she had a damn good laugh on her. Although I found her stealing difficult to deal with, times such as these took the edge of the harshness of life. It wasn't so much a moral objection that kept me honest, or the fear of getting caught, it was also the humiliation of being apprehended in public. But eventually I had to agree that if neither of us could prostitute ourselves, then theft was the only way we'd be able to access money.

We decided to burgle a house, although I suppose it was Jan who decided and I didn't argue. We wandered through the quiet weekday residential streets of Windsor and Balaclava looking for a likely mark. I might have agreed to the plan, but I vetoed every place Jan targeted as suitable, because my heart wasn't really in it. My excuses were endless. The place was too open, too poor looking, too lived in or too vacant looking until, in the end, Jan took charge and proceeded to enter a house through an unlocked side window. I watched her backside disappear over the sill and waited in silence. I was supposed to keep watch. Watch for what? I was in a narrow lane at the side of the house and, by the time I saw anyone they would also have seen me, and I wouldn't be too hard to catch. Not only was I a failure as a thief, I also had no idea how to act as a lookout and, when I thought she'd been in the house forever my nerve gave out.

'Jan, Jan, hurry up. I think I can hear someone.'

There was no response from inside the house. I'd been abandoned once again with my fear.

'Come on, Jan. We need to get out of here.'

No answer again. I felt too exposed hanging around outside, so I angled my way through the window, my leg held stiffly behind me. I wandered through the rooms until I came upon Jan searching through the drawers of a dressing table. I urged her again to leave.

'I'm not finished yet.'

It was a strange feeling being inside someone else's house, a sense of entering the forbidden, but it was not as daunting as waiting outside. I had a desultory look around for something to steal, ignoring the shame of my voyeuristic peek into the secrets of a stranger's life, but I had no idea what to look for or even what to steal. I decided there wasn't much to take.

I never did understand the excitement attached to committing crime. Conversations at Winlaton all centred on crime. Sex and crime, as each girl tried to outdo the other in feats of daring and depravity. I couldn't see any glory in the pain of getting in and out a window and trespassing with intent. The bounty was small, a few items of clothing and an assortment of costume jewellery at the most, while the risks were great. Just how great I was to find out as I checked the street before leaving the property. There was no movement to the left and nothing of concern to the right, except for a sign denoting the purpose of the building next door as it waved in the breeze; *Balaclava Police Station*. How had we missed that? But such were the things legends are made of and, once we were safely clear of the area, we amused ourselves thinking about the high position we'd hold on the Winlaton honour roll. Exploits of this magnitude this spawned institutional folklore.

But small-time burgs didn't put food in our bellies or a roof over our heads, and I had to accept I was out of my depth trying to survive on the streets of Melbourne. Every day was a test of wit and cunning; and my wit and cunning were both very weary. One day, in a moment of sheer desperation, I made a reverse phone call to my mother. She was surprisingly calm about the situation and encouraged me to phone her friend, the erstwhile Methodist minister who'd deposited me in Regent House two years before. I wanted more than ever to get back to Tasmania, regardless of what it held in store for me, but I didn't trust the minister to organise this.

We continued to sleep in hunger-filled discomfort in parked cars and wake ourselves up under the icy water of toilet block wash basins, wandering aimlessly in search of food handouts and a solution to our homelessness. There were no welfare agencies, apart from the system we were trying to escape from, and neither of us considered turning ourselves in to the police. We'd long since abandoned the idea one of us might earn succour through prostitution, so we looked for other opportunities.

One night we befriended a couple of young blokes, who took pity on us, inviting us back to the bungalow they shared in the backyard of their sister's home. They had to sneak us in, but it was worth it just to glean some sense of ordinariness from having a temporary roof over our head. One of the boys had studied first aid and the odour from the open wounds on my leg, competed with the kerosene fumes from the heater it rested on, drawing his attention. I'd grown somewhat used to the pain by now, and I think the extreme cold had killed off most of the bacteria, but I shared his shock at the state of it once it had been bathed. The main injury was a pulpy mass of exposed flesh, with lesser skin tears around it. He dressed it with a fresh bandage and this, added to the luxury of sleeping in a bed for the first time in almost two weeks, was sheer bliss.

Although I had to share a bed with my Good Samaritan, I was assured of an unmolested good night's sleep, as the image he had of my reeking leg was a definite passion killer. Unfortunately Jan, who lacked the same putrid deterrent, spent the entire night fighting off the advances of her amorous bed partner. I drifted off to sleep to the sounds of her grunted rejections and woke to more of the same. Both young men had to leave early the next morning to go to work, cautioning us to be quiet, and not let anyone see us leave. We set about making a silent breakfast and took turns to luxuriate in a hot bath. I was reluctant to leave this haven, but the boys had given us directions out of Melbourne and onto the highway leading out of the city toward Shepparton, and we needed to make a start. It wasn't where I wanted to go, but Jan assured me we'd able to stay at her mother's house. My plan was to use that as a base, get a job, and save for my plane fare out of the state.

I turned on the hot water tap over the bath for a last surge of warmth when an angry voice rent the air.

'I don't know who you are, but you can come out of there, right now!'

Us? Was this person talking to us? We had been so quiet no-one could possibly have known we were in here. Jan and I looked at each other, two sets of eyes bulging in fear of detection.

'Come out of there, now, or I'll call the police!'

I was out of the bath in a flash and dragging my clothes over my still damp body, fearful the owner of the angry voice would burst in. Jan gathered our few belongings together and we debated in an urgent whisper over who should reply to the voice. I lost.

'We're coming out now. I just need to get dressed first.'

'Well you'd better make it snappy, whoever you are.'

I could hear the mutterings of other voices in the background and the bark of a dog. I wondered if I was destined to be followed through life by angry women and their canine companions.

Jan opened the door and pushed me in front of her into the white glare of the winter morning. Our outraged proxy host stood some distance away, hands on ample hips, words spilling from her equally ample mouth.

'Get out of here right now you filthy sluts. I should call the police.'

Her respectable companions nodded in agreement and the small terrier shook and yelped with each furious word, a low growl that belied its miniature size. Jan and I walked up the path towards the gate as the woman continued to hurl abuse at us, Mrs Suburbia at her obscene best. Her comments were scathing and conveyed her opinion of us as something less than human. The dog meanwhile, wearying of its tough guy role, approached us with its tail wagging, tongue waving in an offer of friendship. She called him back several times, her face showing her puzzlement at his disloyalty to the cause.

'Come here, boy, you don't know what you'll catch off them.' And then she laughed at her cleverness and her audience tittered their agreement as we walked, heads bowed in shame, away from her hospitality. The cleanliness I'd gained from my bath stripped away by the implication of her words.

It was mid-afternoon before we reached the highway on the outskirts of the city, as we agreed there was no point trying to hitchhike until we were beyond the reach of regular police highway patrols. We'd skirted the city and walked through the outer suburbs, watching other people with ordinary lives going about their everyday business. I was envious. Normal was all I'd ever aspired to. I'd only ever wanted to be ordinary and blend with life.

There's a sense of exposure when hitch hiking, of being open to the scrutiny of drivers who can assess, at a glance, a person's worthiness to enter their vehicle or their potential as a partner for casual sex. I was not unaware of the dangers of hitching and, while Jan was less wary, she was as selective as I was in what rides we accepted. We walked backwards, facing the oncoming traffic, in order to make a quick assessment whether to extend our thumb or alter our gait to a casual stroll. My limp worked to our advantage in gaining a sympathetic response from families, and it was a deterrent for those of the prowl.

Three rides later we rumbled into Shepparton, exiting appreciatively from the high cab of a road transporter. Jan was excited to be in her home town, but it was an alien landscape to me, built on a flat plain and dominated by fruit canneries. I was, however, eager to get to Jan's mother's house where, she'd assured me, we'd both be made welcome.

The reality was something else again.

We entered the ramshackle cottage by the back doorway. The door was off its hinges and had to lifted to one side to allow entry, then returned to its position against the door frame in paradoxical security. Her mother lived in this tumble-down dwelling, the decaying remnant of what had been Jan's family home before the vibrancy had been stripped from it with her father's death, ten years earlier, and his wife's entry in to the confused world of Alzheimer's in the years that followed. Her ten older siblings had migrated to other towns and cities as soon as they'd left school, eager to be gone from the stranger who'd taken their mother's place.

Most of the furnishings had been stripped from the house and cooking facilities were non-existent. The bath was housed in a decrepit shed in the weed infested back yard, but we managed to light the old wood chip heater at the end of the rusting tub, taking turns to keep watch for the movement of spiders and insects. This was my first encounter with a water-heating device of this nature and although it coughed and spluttered and spat hot ash at irregular intervals, I was grateful for the cleansing water. Despite the shortcomings of the shanty accommodation, I felt safe enough to relax my guard against police apprehension. I'd planned to use Jan's house as an address so I could get a job, save some money and go back to Tasmania, but the cycle of homelessness was to continue in the parochial and small town attitudes of 1960 Shepparton. In this rural backwater an address was synonymous with reputation, and offers of employment were not forthcoming.

Jan resumed her relationship with her old boyfriend and I tagged along as an unwilling appendage. During the day we wandered the streets in a fruitless search for the miracle that would change our lives, hanging out on the periphery of those on the fringe of society themselves; always outside looking in. We heard about a live-in position in Kyabram, looking after two children while their mother was in hospital. We seized this as the opportunity for a new beginning.

Kyabram was a small town twenty minutes by road from Shepparton and a generation in time away from the rest of the world. The position Jan and I were to share was at a farmhouse occupied by Hughie, a sixty-one year old farm hand, his twenty-one year old wife, and their three year old son and an infant daughter. The wife suffered from leg ulcers and needed hospital care.

The other occupant of the house was an aging Aboriginal named Jacky Bond, an ex-rodeo rider who had a penchant for grappa, a drink with a high alcohol content produced locally by Italian fruit growers. Jacky Bond shared a room with an assortment of broken tools and other items gleaned from the local tip, a bicycle frame he intended to restore this year or the next, and the overflow from the colony of mice that inhabited the abandoned kitchen. He slept on the wooden floor with an assortment of old coats and other rags for covering.

Jan and I shared a double bed in a room that had a pine wall to Dado-height and above this, hessian covered with wallpaper extended to the high ceiling. This was all that separated us from the room next door Hughie shared with his wife and children. The wall had tears in the paper where the hessian showed through and, on many occasions, Hughie's aging eye could also be seen angled through the open weave.

Our only duties were to tend to the children, sad pale-faced waifs who ate sparingly of the meagre offerings. No meals were prepared in the kitchen, where hundreds of mice ran up and down the walls, over every surface and through the unwashed dishes of meals past. This room, its furniture and utensils, had been used in cohabitation with the rodents, until the housewife eventually ceded defeat and simply shut the door on the whole filthy mess.

One day, early in our stay, and in a moment of shared optimism, Jan and I decided we might be able to re-take control of this room. Then we'd be able to use the old wood stove to provide more nutritious meals for the children, and we'd have pots and pans and crockery and utensils for everyday use. It was a short lived ambition. The flurry of mice when we opened the door, their defiance in the face of our intrusion, and the sheer enormity of the mess and junk in the room to be sorted out made us both shudder in defeat. We left the room to the victors and the door remained firmly shut.

The family's diet consisted of chunks of bread and butter, and their only meat was cheap sausages or hot dogs cooked on a pan over the open fire. Hughie's remuneration, from his casual employment on a nearby farm, was free rent in the derelict farmhouse and fresh milk daily. When there was no food, the wife bound her legs in scraps of material and solicited assignations with the scions of the local cockies, who paid for her services with tobacco and butter and other grocery items.

For our assistance to the family, Jan and I received free board and food when it was available. The antiseptic environment of the institution, and the devout worship of disinfectant, left us both with an obsessive need for cleanliness and Jan and I began our duties with diligence and enthusiasm. We scrubbed and cleaned our way through the house to make a more hygienic environment for the children and ourselves. It was a huge undertaking, and we only ever completed our own bedroom and the general living area, before ceding to the unmovable presence of the mice and the daily trail of mud carried in on Hughie's and Jacky Bond's gumbooted feet. We then directed our energies into cleaning the children. We found the bath under a pile of rubble and decades of dirt and looked at each other in despair when we realised it had no other connection with the house other than its location under its roof. There were no taps or other signs of plumbing, and no outlet drain. We settled on an old bucket as the only receptacle capable of holding water to sponge bath the baby and sluice down the older child, using this same bucket to wash in the privacy of our bedroom, one ear tuned to the sound of entry into the house and both eyes on the alert for Hughie, the elderly voyeur.

The only benefit from this accommodation was the respite it gave us from the anxiety of looking over our shoulder for the police, and the constant wait for the hand of apprehension on those same shoulders. Life down on the farm was boring in the extreme and more so after the wife came home and took over the care of her children, a feat she somehow managed from the comfort of her chair at the side of the fireplace. Occasionally she'd venture into the town to visit the doctor and to solicit some business for herself. When she suggested I visit the local hospital because my leg looked ulcerated, I was more than ready and willing to go. I'd almost forgotten about it. My tolerance to pain had increased and I'd learnt to compensate for the limitations it placed on my mobility. I was very alarmed at the thought of leg ulcers, but even more concerned about using the horse and cart as a mode of transport into town. I didn't want to attract undue attention, but I was assured this was the usual means of travel in the country so I acquiesced.

We bounced and jostled as the high wheels negotiated the rutted tracks leading from the farm to the highway, our backsides jolting in rhythm with the clopping of the horse as it trotted purposefully toward civilization. The nearer we came to the township of Kyabram, the more my earlier sense of unease returned, as cars whizzed past and the horse shied in their wake.

'Are you sure everyone else travels by horse and cart?'

'Yeah, I told ya that. Everyone does it.'

The wife hitched her soiled skirt above her stumpy scarred legs, the better to display her wares, flicking the reins expertly.

As we passed houses on the outskirts of town, people paused in their daily tasks and stared after us with looks of amusement on their faces. Neat cottages set behind clipped hedges and green lawns, bordered the highway and housewives in floral pinnies watched our progress with wide-eyed amusement. I tried to hide from their scrutiny, slinking down in the cart, but there was no place to hide. My self-consciousness was disrupted by the sound of children's voices, that heralded our approach to a school. The open expanse of a playing field came alive with the rush of small bodies as they ran towards to boundary fence where they laughed and pointed at this relic from the past and its unlikely occupants.

'Other people don't use a horse and cart, do they?'

The wife had gone conveniently deaf, her jaw set in a solid line as she stared straight ahead, clicking her tongue and flicking the reins in unison.

'They don't do my washin' so what's it matter, we'll be gettin' out soon anyhow.' With an expert 'whoa', she brought the horse to a halt at the rear of an old garage. A red sign at the front proclaimed it as a Mobil service station, while the side of the building still bore the faded signage of Anderson's Livery. Anxious to divorce ourselves from this person who was so ill regarded, Jan and I arranged to meet up with her later for the ride home.

Kyabram was a small town and it didn't take us long to reach the hospital, only to find there was no doctor on the premises. A kind hearted nurse tutted over my leg, put on a fresh bandage, and urged me to have it treated as soon as possible, making an appointment for me to see the doctor when he had his next clinic, before we made our leisurely way back to meet the wife. Jan stopped in every shop along the way and added items to her wardrobe, plus matching accessories, while I stood watch outside and waited for the weight of apprehension to fall on me.

Back at the farmhouse disenchantment settled over us once more. Jan missed her boyfriend, who could only make it across to see her a couple of times a week, and I was disillusioned with the inability to change my life situation. I was no closer to getting home than I'd been when I was in Winlaton. I was disgusted with the hovel we were living in and afraid, if I stayed too long, I'd begin to accept this life as my own normality. The wife's eye had joined with Hughie's at his pervert post and I was concerned where their interest might take them.

The next time Jan's boyfriend came to visit he took us back to Shepparton with him. Her mother's shanty seemed pristine after the Kyabram experience. Our lives returned to the rut of nothingness. The only change came when I sought medical attention at the Mooroopna Base Hospital for my leg, giving some structure to our existence as we walked the short distance between the two towns each day for my treatment.

We'd met some kids who lived in the local housing commission area and they appeared to accept us for whom and what we were. Some nights we invited ourselves to their houses, always sensitive to existing relationships and dynamics, not wanting to cause enmity for ourselves. Jan's situation was different from mine. She was one of them, a local, who had a boyfriend from a family well regarded in the area. I came from Tasmania, a place far distant from their limited experience of life and people. Other differences were clearly marked by the thick tattoos on my arms, the fresh wounds on my legs interwoven with scars, and my unfamiliarity with their dialect and small town customs.

The nights we stayed home were also a problem, as we huddled under thin bedding and old clothes to ward off the cold. There were many nights when we had to get up and move around just to keep warm; nights when our hunger was so acute it united with our external discomfort, and we sought respite in creative diversion. On these occasions we'd put on every item of clothing from our meagre wardrobe and wander the streets on the lookout for an opportunity to obtain food, hunter gatherers of the night. In desperation borne of hunger, Jan suggested we break into the primary school canteen and I didn't argue against the plan.

We broke a window to gain access and I took up my usual watching position while Jan filled our bags with food. Once again I was to find she was not a very skilled thief when, after removing ourselves from the vicinity of the school, we rested in a large drain to divide the spoils. I suppose there was some analogy of natural justice between our situation, which had led us to seek respite from the cold, and Jan's selection of cartons of ice creams. These were already beginning to melt, despite the low temperature, so we set about eating as many as we could before they disappeared completely. I managed to consume a carton of Eskimo Pies on my own, while Jan made short work of the Choc Wedges. The other proceeds from the theft, boxes of chocolate freckles and wrapped sweets, we repacked into our bags. Warmed by the sugar hit, we made our boisterous way home through the silent night streets of Shepparton.

With our energy levels bolstered by another overdose of sugar, we set out the following night seeking diversion from the cold. Hapless and hopeless thieves, we had no idea where to go, what to do or who to rob until, just before the night air turned into pre-dawn chill, we saw it. It was one of the few times Jan and I agreed on anything, but it was love at first sight for both of us; an elegant concrete garden stork about one metre high, with a bowl at its base forming a bird bath. We decided the bowl would be the perfect receptacle for the lolly wrappers that had the potential to over-run our small veranda bedroom. The beginning of the nesting extinct, perhaps.

After a few days, we began to tire of our Freckles and Fantale diet, and offered some of our bounty up to the local youths to try and purchase entry into their world. In return for our gifts we were invited to a party the following Saturday night. I liked the feeling of acceptance and began to think more generously about the town. Maybe things would look up now. With contacts I could get a job, have a life even.

The party was held in the housing commission area of Shepparton. I was shy amongst these strangers and didn't take much notice when there was a loud knocking at the front door, until someone called out.

'Cops! It's the cops!'

Jan and I fled out the back door and over the fence, running blind in the darkness of the night and our panic. I found it difficult to keep up with her and modified my flight to a slow limp, alert for the sounds of pursuit. A beam of light from a torch threatened to expose us and Jan pulled me to the ground, but it was uneven and I missed my footing, taking us both down a steep incline into a pit, where broken bottles and discarded cans caught at my clothes and my skin.

'Ouch! Oh Jesus, it's a bloody rubbish dump.'

'Just shut up for God's sake, or they'll find us.'

Jan pulled me down and shushing me with threats of detection. We lay there, blended with the trash of other people's lives as the police hunted for us in the long grass, and for a long time after the torch beams and voices died away. I was disappointed my brief acceptance into society had been interrupted before it had a chance to begin and I was embarrassed by my fugitive state.

'Come on, they've gone now. Let's go back to the party. We'll be safe because the cops'll never expect us to go back there.'

'But they might. Let's just go home.'

Jan wasn't happy, but we were both looking and smelling the worse for wear so she agreed to go home and clean up first.

I saw them as we turned the corner. The divvy van parked under the street light out the front of Jan's mother's house, another police car in the driveway, and a flurry of blue uniforms moving in and out of the verandah bedroom. From our hiding spot we watched as two police officers carried our stork out and put it in the back of the van, while others carried the opened cartons of sweets. Our entire food supply had been raided and confiscated.

I sensed the end of my freedom coming closer. In the meantime, we still had our newfound friends, so we returned to the scene of the party, although the people weren't as welcoming as they'd been earlier. They gathered in small groups, whispering together, and I decided to leave. I was surprised when they tried to persuade me to stay.

'Don't go. The cops'll get ya if you leave now.'

But I was edgy. The police had already been once, so they could just as easily come again and I wasn't sure who they were really after. I looked around the room at this representation of the youth of Shepparton, clad as they were in the fashion of seasons past. These greasy haired boys and stony faced girls didn't look the type to attract police attention, but I didn't know or trust them. I continued towards the door, ignoring their outstretched arms, and then the knock came again; the urgent knock of police on the scent. Jan and I ran to the back of the house, only to find our exit barred by one of our new friends. Then the police were in the house, their voices authoritative, demanding to know where we were. I ducked into the nearest room and dived under the bed, competing for space with discarded clothes and other clutter, as I huddled with my back against the wall. The heavy footsteps drew nearer.

'Come on out now, the game's up.'

I watched as the light beams from their torches crisscrossed, miniature search lights feeling their way down and under the bed. The light reflected off my suspenders, exposed when my skirt rode up during my attempt to evade capture.

It was over.

I was paraded past the noble citizens in their suburban colosseum, my arm bent sharply up my back to immobilize me, hard knuckles of the law thrust into my flesh. I made the token struggle. It was important to satisfy the audience. A swish of the hips and shake of the head and a few 'fuck youse' and then I found myself face down on the bonnet of the divvy van, my cheek bone smarting from the forced contact with the cold metal, my arm forced at an unnatural angle against my shoulder blades.

I conceded defeat.

Jan proved a harder animal to trap as she struggled against the loss of freedom. She had more to lose than I did. This was her town, her boyfriend, and everything she knew was in this place. It was her life; however, within a short space of time she'd also been subdued and thrown in the back of the van with me. As we were driven to Shepparton police station, she whispered her next plan of escape. I didn't want to know. I'd had enough and for me it was over.

We spent the night in the filth of the police cells. Dimly lit concrete blocks that held the memory of a century of blood, vomit, excreta and urine of previous occupants. We shared a cell with a woman prisoner waiting transport to Fairlea Women's Prison in Melbourne to begin a sentence for grievous bodily harm with a knife. This woman had a menacing presence and I felt vulnerable to attack from her.

After a sleepless night, a cold water wash, and a lukewarm metal mug of black tea we began our journey back to Melbourne. The escorting police officer had decided to make it a family day and piled his wife and children into the back of the police sedan, to share the space with the female prisoner. Jan and I were handcuffed together and placed in the front seat with the driver.

It's a long way from Shepparton to Melbourne and the officer stopped for a rest break. He, with his respectably neat wife and children, went into the police residence at Seymour for morning tea and a visit, while Jan and I and the other prisoner were placed in the old lockup, a single cell building left over from colonial times. We were kept handcuffed to each other, and all the time Jan whispered to me to escape at the first opportunity once we were on the road again.

'When the car slows at the traffic lights I'm off.'

'Well, I'm not! I've had enough of running, and we're handcuffed together.'

She threatened to drag me with her from the car and I threatened to hold on to the police officer to strengthen my hold. She called me a bitch and other such words and I called her a fucking idiot. She dared me with her eyes each time the car slowed, and I dared her back, until eventually we pulled into the cavernous indoor car park of Russell Street police station in Melbourne.

We were back.

Goodbye Welfare

Within hours of my arrival back in Winlaton it was as if I'd never left. For the first time I actually enjoyed the re-admission bath, phenol and all, the first really decent bath I'd had since my escape seven weeks earlier. At least I didn't have to look over my shoulder, and the only perverts were the staff who were paid to watch young girls take a bath, their interest solely taken up with matters of procedure and security.

Then I was back in my room again. No bed. No communication. But I didn't care. The last two months of living rough had taken their toll on me. I had bronchitis and a high fever, and I shivered throughout my first day back in a delirium of extreme body temperatures, huddled on the wooden floor in of my punishment. That evening the section chief decided, due to my poor state of health, I should be allowed to have a bed in the room during the day. The pay-off for this was to be an additional day's isolation. It turned out I was in isolation for even longer than expected as the bronchitis compressed my chest and fed my fever, but this was only a temporary respite from the games and manipulations of the section.

I'd never been charged with any offence, nor received a set sentence, and I still had no idea what the length of my stay in Winlaton would be. I only knew that not many girls remained beyond their seventeenth birthday and even fewer stayed after they turned eighteen. As I was now only a few months short of my seventeenth birthday, this should have given me some assurance, but the future was never clear in this place. For many girls, Winlaton was simply the gateway to gaol, while for others, their release was nothing more than an admission to a mental health facility, an asylum. This was the most dreaded destination, as the likelihood of release from of one of those places was very remote. Before my last absconding I'd tried to get a date as to when I might be released, but there was never an answer. Somehow I'd become lost in this punitive system. A number before a name. A problematic statistic.

Whether it was my ill health and depleted energy or some other reason but while I was in isolation, I'd made a decision to conform in every way. I was tired through to my soul and I determined to follow every rule, no matter how senseless it might seem, and to keep quiet in the face of provocation. I faced the next medical without a murmur of protest, finally understanding submission would be my only chance of real and lasting escape from the system. Maybe I was growing up.

The attempts at creating mischief began while I was still in my room, with girls breaking away from their escorts in the age old fashion, running up to my door with their childish messages intended to intimidate.

Who were these people anyway?

They were all strangers to me and would remain so.

'We're gunna get you when you get out.'

'Fuck off!' I'd been down this road too many times now to play their silly games. Let them rape and bash and befoul some other silly bugger because it wasn't going to be me.

Once I'd been released from my room I noticed some subtle changes to section life. We now had an elderly lady come in once a week to reach us craft. What a brave woman she was to continue coming to this hellhole, week after thankless week, dragging her pieces of felt and fluff and stuffing to be transformed into pink poodles and blue bears. And if she did most of the sewing herself for these ham fisted young women, what did it really matter? It was a diversion.

Another change was the introduction of floor mats and bedspreads that coincided with a visit from journalists who worked for various Melbourne newspapers; a temporary luxury that was gathered up and removed once the press had left the institution. Often girls who'd been released would go to the Truth, a newspaper with a reputation for reporting on the most sensational and salacious stories, and tell them what was happening to girls behind the barbed wire fence. Because we were not allowed to have newspapers or magazines, or listen to news broadcasts, we never knew the outcome, if any, of these reports. There was always a rumour of investigations pending, and threats made to staff they'd be reported to the Truth, but none of us were any the wiser for this.

The only inkling we had that information about our treatment had reached beyond the walls was on a few occasions when staff would bustle around with worried looks on their faces and a clean-up would be ordered. Shining floors were scrubbed even shinier, walls washed and girl's mouths sanitized under threat of more severe punishment, and we'd know an inspection was imminent. Floor rugs and bedspreads were brought in to soften the image of Goonyah, and all internal doors left open while the delegation of departmental heads, politicians and newspaper reporters were in the section; a pretence of low security and homeliness.

Naturally no girl was kept in isolation during the visit. We were instructed how to behave, and bribed accordingly, with the suggestion that the show conditions might be allowed to remain if we demonstrated we knew how to behave ourselves properly. The most presentable girls, and those most amenable to bribery, were selected to answer pre-approved questions, and the delegation left, satisfied our living conditions were as stated by the department. Any girls assessed as unpredictable and unbribable, such as myself, were escorted around the institution, always one section away from the eyes and ears of the visitors.

When the proposed improvements to section life were not forthcoming, the staff placed the blame with the government of the day and we would all mutter for the next few days about 'bloody Rylah', the then Premier of Victoria.

'Miss, can I write a letter?'

'You've already written one this week.'

'Yes – but.'

'No, it's against the rules.'

'Ahh, that bloody Rylah.'

And so it went.

One change that did remain was the introduction of weekly ballet classes for all the sections. Goonyah girls were escorted every Friday evening to the big rec on Karingal section, where we'd change into royal blue bloomers and second hand ballet slippers. What a sight we made. As with the communal section clothes, where distribution made no concession to different body shapes or sizes, big backsides were squashed into the smaller sizes; folds of flesh pushing at seams and elastic cutting into beefy thighs, while their opposites got lost in the larger sizes, billowing around shapeless bottoms, while stick thin legs jutted from loose elastic.

Once in our uniform we formed a circle and an old lady with a walking cane, accompanied by an elderly pianist, began the lesson. We warmed up by running in a circle, toes pointed, around the perimeter of the room. I hated the futility and inappropriateness of this activity. I understood the charity behind the action, but none of us belonged in the world of ballet. We didn't belong in any activity attached to polite society, but it did get me out of Goonyah for an hour a week.

I developed the habit of sitting out the lesson behind the piano. At least that way I couldn't get dragged into someone else's problems if they decided to misbehave. It worked out well for me. I joined the group at the beginning of the session, and then broke free once my position in the circle was at the far side of the room near the piano, where I sat between the piano and the wall. I joined back in at the end of the session when the closing circle formed to dance our way out of the room. This worked well until one week when, just as I re-joined the circle, I looked up to see Miss Doran sitting near the door. I couldn't believe my bad luck. I'd almost succeeded in becoming invisible in the weeks since my return, and now I was going to get into trouble without even trying. I decided to avoid her eyes and threw all of my enthusiasm into my exit routine, sailing past her without even a glance.

'Merlene, come over here please.'

I wanted to pretend not to hear her, but there was no point. I'd been caught out and I'd just have to wear it. My shoulders slumped as I walked towards her, my dancer's poise quickly discarded.

'Yes, Miss Doran. Did you want me?'

'Yes, I did dear, how would you like to go home?'

I looked at her in astonishment. Go home? What did that mean? And what did it matter where they sent me as long as it was away from this place?

'I've had a phone call from your mother and she'd like you to go back home.'

I tried to take in what she was saying. My mother wanted me home after all these months. Was that all it took for me to be released from this place - a phone call from my mother?

'Of course there are a few conditions.'

'When will I leave?'

'I can't tell you that, and you'll have to stay on Goonyah until you leave. You're too great a security risk to transfer to an open section.'

'But I'd never abscond if I knew I was getting out. Why would I?'

I could see she didn't understand and it didn't matter anyway. I wondered who had rang whom. It didn't make any sense that suddenly, out of the blue, my mother would phone and ask for my release. I suspected it had been Miss Doran who'd made the contact, most likely when I'd been returned by the police and I was so unwell but, however it happened, I was going home. I was going to be free, legally free, and I didn't let myself think beyond that.

'There's one condition, though. You have to sign a paper saying you won't come back to Victoria for at least two years.'

'I'll sign my life away of it will help me get out of this place.'

'I don't think you'll need to go that far,' she laughed at my enthusiasm, 'now get back to your section.'

The days passed with no word of when I might be leaving, but I trusted Miss Doran and knew it would happen soon. I noticed the staff had begun to treat me differently and didn't try to provoke me anymore, or maybe they'd found more receptive targets for their boredom. I went about my everyday business and hid my impatience to be free. I did my chores as asked, sitting out the idle hours in the rec room, and attending craft sessions when I was allowed. I was just putting the finishing touches to a small felt poodle when I was told I was needed in the store room. I tried to question the staff escorting me as to the purpose of this request, but she only parroted the order again.

'You're wanted in the store, that's all I know.'

She knocked on the store room door and handed me over to the staff in charge, who instructed me to remove all of my clothes and get dressed from the pile of clothing laid out on the table. Underwear, suspenders and stockings, all new but very dated, a twin set and pleated skirt, and second hand black court shoes. This outfit of daggy respectability contrasted with the tattoos that peeped below the ribbed sleeve bands of the cardigan, and it didn't match in any way the person I wanted to be.

I was handed a box containing the clothes I'd been wearing when I was picked up by the police seven months before, and asked to check and sign receipt of the contents. My patent leather purse was emptied and the amount tallied against the admission entry. I had come in with one pound ten shillings and the purse held only ten shillings. I signed anyway. I was then handed my 'pay' for the seven months I'd been in Winlaton. Once all the deductions had been made for misdemeanours and alleged breaches of rules my earnings amounted to eighteen shillings. I signed for this also. I peeled the sticker off my purse that had my name and the words, *Ward of the State of Victoria* and my ward number on it, as the door was unlocked and I was released from the institution. Two officers drove me to Essendon Airport for my flight home to Tasmania.

The Final Escape

She stood alone at the wooden railing that separated the tarmac from the airport car park. From a distance she looked small and unthreatening but, as I drew closer, she squared her shoulders and grew in height and strength. I wondered if this was a defence against the whole world or only me. Hooking the band of my cardigan in my thumbs I pulled it down to cover any exposed tattoos. The black marks that looked so ordinarily in place within the institution now looked common. They were the marks of an undesirable. I knew I'd have to tell my mother about the tattoos at some stage, but my fear of her had returned on sight and I was concerned her reaction might be to send me back to Winlaton, or worse.

Our greeting was stilted. I'd lost the ability to gabble to cover such awkwardness and she'd never had it in the first place, but I made an effort.

'How're the little ones?'

'They're fine.'

'How's Dad?'

'He's okay.'

I knew she wanted me to ask about her. To ask how she was, and then she'd talk non-stop recounting her many ailments, specialist appointments, and the hospital stays that had occurred since I left. I couldn't ask this though. It was too intimate and signified a caring of which I was incapable. I knew whatever illnesses she'd experienced during my absence would be attributed to me, silently accusing with that pained and long suffering look, designed to elicit the feelings of guilt she derived much of her power from.

It was an alien feeling to walk back into a life where everyone had lived on in my absence, like returning from the dead when the deceased had never been mourned. The house looked and smelt the same and yet it was unfamiliar to me. I'd lived in confined and controlled spaces, spending hours and days with only my own thoughts for company, and here were these children, the little ones, grown taller and now strangers to me. There was so much to get used to. Doors without locks I could open without asking permission, the freedom to go to the toilet without an escort. And decisions. I could make decisions as to where I sat, what I read, and what I ate, but I had no idea where to begin.

Within a short time of arriving home the excited babble of the children drove me back into myself. I'd had enough freedom for the moment. My mother showed a rare insight and suggested I might want to go upstairs for a while, telling me my bedroom was now the smaller of the two attic rooms and I didn't have to share it with anyone else. The room I entered was very different from the last time I'd seen it. Everything in it was new and the lino, bedspread, walls and accessories were all pink, my favourite colour. Dominating this space, angled from the corner of the room was a Queen Anne style single bed, polished to perfection. My mother, the same mother who never came up the stairs to the attic, had done this for me, and I had to reach deep within myself to find a response. She was downstairs now, waiting for my reaction; to see my appreciation of her efforts, but I felt nothing. Only a few hours ago I'd been sitting in Goonyah, sewing pieces of felt together and now I had my freedom and an opportunity to make a new start and I didn't know how to do it.

I'd lost the ability to feel a long time ago. I knew I'd have to pretend, and that's what I did. I went back down the stairs and thanked my mother, toadying in my performance, and lost myself in a disassociate oration of future intention.

'Thank you. I love it. I know I don't deserve it. I'll be good from now on. I promise.' I meant the words as I spoke them. It was what I wanted, to be a nice girl with nice clothes and a nice bedroom, to be able to blend in with other people. I didn't want to be different. I never had. I only ever wanted to be the same as everyone else, but how could that ever be when I'd had experiences I could never share with anyone.

It doesn't matter how you dress it, lamb will always be lamb, and many times I'd heard my mother say you can't make a silk purse out of a sow's ear. I could swathe my arms in bandages to cover the tattoos. I could cover my scarred legs, but I would still be the same tattooed, scarred person underneath; the common girl who'd been sent away from home so many times. I was still the girl who'd been in the reformatory and who'd mixed with thieves and prostitutes and the mad, bad and sad. The mire of those experiences would always be with me. It would be what other people saw, no matter how much I, or my mother, sought to disguise it.

Within a few days of my arrival home, past patterns of behaviour began to emerge. Unused to the chatter of children and the less regimented life of the family, I found it difficult to communicate at an appropriate or acceptable level. I sought my own company and took refuge in my room, deemed anti-social because I had no idea of social norms. My mother spoke to me about getting a job, but I was afraid of further change. I needed time to adjust.

I found the courage to show my mother the tattoos and she was saddened and ashamed by the ugly markings. She thought I could burn them off with caustic soda and instructed me to dip a flake in water and wipe it across the tattoos. I laid a stream of caustic water across three tattoos before the burning began. The searing pain cut into my flesh as the caustic found its own direction eating through unmarked skin and continuing its journey through the derma and beyond.

At least now I had a valid reason for wearing bandages.

I was sent off to see another of my father's Mason friends who was the personnel officer at Paton's and Baldwin's, a woollen mill that dominated the southern quarter of the city. I stepped outside of myself, as I did whenever I had to deal with the normal functions of life and went through the motions of an interview.

'I'll put you in a nice part of the mill, where there's a better class of girl. It can be hard for girls like you from good families to mix with the more common workers here.'

The pretend Merlene nodded and said thank you and felt comforted by the bandages that hid her own commonness.

'What did you do to your hand?'

'Oh, I just burnt it. It's nearly better. I just keep it covered so I don't get anything in it.'

'Are you sure? I could give you another week before you start work if you want.'

I was tempted to accept his offer of time, but I knew the longer I put it off the harder it would be to make myself walk through the factory doors to begin work. I'd also realized each time I forced myself to do something I was afraid of, or lacked confidence to see through, it became easier the next time. My social skills were very low, I had poor eye contact, and could not initiate or maintain a conversation for any length of time.

The mill worked on a shift work basis. Six in the morning to two in the afternoon one week, and two to ten the next. This was vastly different from my previously ordered life and my body clock remained inflexible to the irregular hours. On the weeks I had the early shift I set off to work after only a couple of hours sleep. I had to leave home very early in the morning to get a lift with Dad on his way to the clean the town hall. I preferred the long walk across town to catching the mill bus, because I was too self-conscious to get on with all of the other women, so well-known to each other, but strangers to me. I'd see them converging down Thistle Street each morning, head scarves over hair rollers, laughing and jostling each other in the dawn light. I wanted so much to be part of a group like this, to be a functioning part of life, but I had no idea where to begin.

The transient life I'd lived throughout my teenage years, a life so very different from my age peers, meant I hadn't been able to form and nurture friendships. I knew people from around the town in a casual, retrospective way, but I didn't know how to reach out and reconnect. And there was Michael who, despite the distance of years and life experience, I had still managed to hold in my heart. My determination to salvage something from the past, to build a positive future, gave me the courage to write to him and we arranged to meet. I allowed myself to look forward with cautious optimism.

Michael and I resumed our relationship from where we'd left it the last time we'd been together. Like pieces of a well-worn jigsaw puzzle we were still able to nestle into each other to make a complete picture. Unfortunately, life had scuffed us both around the edges, leaving gaps in the join, and neither of us knew how to make the pieces stay in place. Our time together alternated between sweet contentment and simmering discontent, and we could find no middle ground or a bridge to span the two extremes. We were both still finding our own way in world of discord, unable to share the burdens life had endowed us with or to make sense of it or each other and yet, confident in the knowledge we loved each other, we persevered. Our best times were when we were alone, without the hindrance of his friends, who brought out the immaturity in him and the insecurity in me, but even then our judgement wasn't always sound. I'd been home for a few weeks, slowly settling into home and employment, and learning about a more normal existence when I had another collision with fate.

Driving around the streets of Launceston with Michael one Saturday afternoon, sharing a long neck of Boag's beer and easy conversation, life seemed too good to be true. Finishing the bottle I asked.

'What will I do with this?' I held it up questioningly. Some boys were fussy about their cars, and where things were placed, so I thought it safer to ask.

'Just chuck it out of the window.'

'Are you sure?'

He'd just turned into St John's Street in the middle of town and I was a bit doubtful. Maybe this was how things were done these days.

'Yeah, just chuck it out of the window.'

I wound the window down and threw it away from the car as he drove. It crashed against the gutter and he sped off. Back in Brisbane Street we parked and talked and watched the world go by, until we were disturbed by a knock on the window and I turned to see a police officer looking in. I froze. Images of other contacts, with other police officers, flashed before me. I could feel the doors closing in on me again. I could hear the key turning in the lock, shutting me off from life once more. Fear grabbed me by the throat and I couldn't speak to answer his questions.

'Who threw the bottle?'

Silence.

'I said who threw that bottle?'

He quickly tired of this one-sided conversation, opened the door and pushed me roughly into the middle of the bench seat.

'Drive to the police station. I'll get some answers there.'

I lit a cigarette, blowing the smoke out the corner of my mouth and causing it to drift in his direction. His sharp slap across my face freed my voice and turned the key to release my noxious self.

'You fucken dirty filthy copper cunt, keep your fucken hands off me.'

He looked at me and smiled, 'That's it. Keep it up. Let's see how many charges I can get you on by the time we get to the station.'

Michael drove in silence, removed from the altercation taking place beside him. This was my life, not his; my problem. Pulling up in the police laneway the officer ordered me from the car, however, before I could move, he reached in and dragged me out by my clothes. I swore at him again and began to walk the few yards to the charge room door, but my progress was halted by his hands on my shoulders and I buckled under the pain as he kneed me in the back of my legs. I sprawled forward onto the tarmac as he released my shoulders, then he grabbed me and repeated the action several more times until I sprawled through the open doorway of the station. The pain behind my knees was unbearable and I was unable to stand. Once inside the small area I was asked my name by other officers, but fear and a sense of helplessness had frozen my voice once again.

'Put her in the cells for a few hours, that'll change her tune.'

They all laughed and the arresting officer twisted my right arm high up my back, causing me to walk on my toes, while another guided me by my left elbow through a doorway and down a set of wide cement steps toward a landing faced by a concrete wall. I felt the gentle pressure on my elbow to steer me down the next flight of steps, but this was lost to the force on my back as the other officer pushed me with such force my face slammed into the concrete wall. My knees, jellied from his previous onslaught, buckled beneath me and I heard a distant ringing in my ears. My face burnt in pain and shame. I don't remember how I got down the last section of steps, nor being placed in a cell; another filthy cell in another filthy gaol.

Was this my true destiny?

I'd had such good intentions, but this hadn't been enough to turn me into a decent person. I was what I'd always been. Rubbish, someone else's trash; a person with no rights and of no consequence.

I had plenty of time to think while I was locked in that cell. I bounced hate around between my head and my heart, and I refused to accept this as my life. I looked at the bars on the windows and compared them to other bars across other windows. I looked inwardly to the barriers that kept me from being the person I wanted to be, and I knew I'd continue to fight for a better life. There had to be a some way to stand up for myself, where I could retain dignity without risk of punishment.

I passed two more hours in reflection, firming this resolve, before the duty officer unlocked the door and told me my father had arrived to bail me out.

'Have you seen your face?'

'No…?'

He led me across the room to where a stained mirror hung above a filthy wash basin, a metaphor for the prisoners who'd stood before it.

'Have a look in this then.'

I looked at the distortion of my face, discolouration shining through the tightened skin.

'You should charge the bloke who did this to you. It's not right. You shouldn't do that to anyone, especially a young girl your age and we don't need coppers like that in the force. Tell them upstairs you want to press charges and I'll speak up for you.'

His words of kindness and support reinforced my new found resolution to set a higher value on myself so, when the inspector asked the standard question about whether I was satisfied with how I'd been treated during my time at the station, and asked me to sign to the affirmative, I declined.

'No, I won't sign it because I wasn't treated well. I want to charge the officer who assaulted me.'

Although I spoke the words clearly, minus the expletives I would have used previously to emphasise my point, I heard my father's shocked intake of breath from behind me. The inspector glared at me as Dad spoke for both of them.

'Don't be silly, girl. You asked for what you got. If you behaved yourself you wouldn't be in this position, so just sign the book and let's get out of here.'

'No. I'm not going to sign it, because it's not true. Just look at my face. I didn't ask for this or anything else to be done to me and I want to press charges.'

The inspector looked at Dad, knowing he had his support in whatever he chose to do with me.

'It's back to the cells with you then, Miss. Let's see if a few more hours down there won't change your mind.'

That's all it took to get me locked up again. I didn't tell the duty officer what had occurred and he averted his eyes when I came back down. It wasn't his fault and I had tried, but some systems can never be challenged or modified in anyway. I'd seen the best and the worst of it that afternoon, however, and it was the best of it that stayed with me during the darkness of early evening as I reviewed my situation. There'd been something in the honesty of the duty officer that gave me hope. If he could see me as being worthy of being treated better, then I needed to find that within myself. I did have a goodness in me I'd always known was there and I needed to find this again, to hold it tight and refuse to let it be taken from me. I resolved once more to take control of my life and never allow my liberty to be taken again. Not ever.

It was a much-relieved father who returned some hours later to bail me out, watching me sign the satisfactory treatment page. He expressed his sentiments as we walked to the car.

'You brought it on yourself, girl, you couldn't go charging the bloke for just doing his job.'

'I didn't bring it on myself. I didn't do anything to deserve to be hurt like that. I threw the bottle out of the car window and I realise now that was wrong, and the court will decide my punishment for that. I blew cigarette smoke in his face and that was rude, but he didn't need to hit me for doing it. I swore at him because he hit me, and the court will also decide my punishment for that. I did nothing to deserve being hit or kneed in the back of the legs and pushed over, or having my face slammed into a concrete wall. I only signed the form because I knew I'd have to stay locked up until I did sign it and I lied by signing it, because I know I wasn't treated at all well by that particular police officer.'

'I just wish you'd learn to stay out of trouble, girl.'

It was four weeks before the case was heard in court. Four weeks for my face to return to normal, and four weeks for the informing officer to resign. I guess he realized he wasn't cut out to be a police officer, after all.

Life developed into another rut after this episode. I went to work, and made good money doing piece work, but I still had no idea how to handle my finances. I paid board to my mother, bought cigarettes, and wasted the rest. I bought clothes I thought would make me look like every other girl, but I always had to guess my size, as I was too self-conscious to try anything on in the shop. Even when I bought shoes, I would try to guess my size. Most of the time this worked out and, when it didn't, I slopped around in shoes with the toes stuffed with toilet paper to stop them from bending up.

I was still too unsure of myself to go into a bank or a chemist shop, or anywhere at all where I had to speak with girls or women who had more confidence than I had, and that covered just about everybody. I didn't know how to talk to normal people and I avoided situations where I might have to do this. In the instances where I had to go into a shop and ask for something, I'd repeat the request over and over in my mind beforehand, rehearsing it until I could say what I needed to without stammering, but even then my face would redden. I'd hang my head and show my inferiority to the world.

Jill had been acquitted of the attempted murder of her father and taken in by a well-to-do local family. I reached back into the past to try and resume this relationship, to bring some ordinariness to two extraordinary lives, but her new 'parents' didn't approve of me, instructing her to tell me the friendship could not continue, that I was not the sort of person she should be associating with. I understood this very well.

Michael and I plodded along, both of us trying to exorcise our demons independent of the other. The only thing we were both certain of was that we loved each other and were destined to be together. We would work it out and get married when I turned eighteen. His best friend was the same boy, who'd been my first boyfriend so many years before. He played us off against each other and we were both too naïve to see beyond the moment. He was a true friend to neither of us and his manipulations took their toll.

My seventeenth birthday came and went. I convinced myself my birth mother would finally come on this day, if only to meet me. Even though I'd given up on her years before, there still remained a small spark of hope. My childhood was almost at an end and I felt that, if I was to remove the question mark that shaded my existence, it had to be this year or never. I went on a pilgrimage to Rocklynn House, where I'd been born, certain she'd be there waiting.

She wasn't.

I waited for a long time but she didn't come.

My brother had become engaged during one of my absences and this, like so many other family events, passed by without my knowledge. My parent's twenty-fifth wedding anniversary had been the last family occasion I'd attended. I'd spent my fifteenth birthday and Christmas at Regent House and my sixteenth in the convent, and I'd missed every other event in between. Despite my resolve to walk tall with dignity, I was still a nervous fledgling, and I became very apprehensive when the wedding day approached. His fiancée had always shown kindness towards me, but it was the social aspect of the occasion that filled me with dread. With no experience of the conventions and etiquette involved, I was particularly concerned about the wedding reception. I'd never eaten in a restaurant and knew nothing about the correct use of multiple cutlery and glasses, nor any of the other social mores I assumed other people took for granted. I was very aware of the image my tattoos gave me and this, combined with my low self-esteem and confidence, created an anxiety I fought desperately to overcome.

I spent considerable time choosing a dress to wear, something that satisfied my own sense of comfort, but would also look respectable. I eventually settled on a safe straight line dress in a navy colour, with a double row of white buttons down the front. I teamed this with white accessories and skin coloured Band-Aids placed at strategic points on my arms and across the scarred tattoo above my right knee. I practiced walking in high heel shoes and experimented with different hair styles, in search of an image I thought might help me pass into polite society.

The day of the wedding came and I, so self-obsessed, had no thought for how the bride or bridegroom might be feeling. My sense of inferiority overwhelmed me and I withdrew further into myself. There was no room for me in the family car. My younger siblings had long since taken over my space in the family so, on the day of the wedding I teetered on high heels, as I walked from the bus stop to the church. My mother had abandoned her need to show family unity after she'd gone public about my placement at Regent House, and she distanced herself and the family from me by several pews. It was from this position of estrangement I witnessed the origin of my mother's religious bigotry as my grandmother whispered and giggled her way through the Nuptial Mass, mocking the customs and traditions of the Catholic Church.

And they were ashamed of me!

I stood alone in the churchyard as the couple emerged, the wall of different life experiences creating a barrier to my participation. I watched in dreamlike fascination and felt a remote envy and sadness knowing I could never expect to have this same respectability or acceptance from family or community. I made a decision not to attend the reception, my presence would only cause discomfort and embarrassment for others and for me.

At home the situation deteriorated further and much of this resulted from my inability to express myself effectively. I wanted to do the right thing, but every good intention turned belly up. It wasn't that my behaviour was wrong, it was more about my attitude. I was so determined no-one was going to disempower me again, I kept everyone at arm's length. I came and went as I pleased; a boarder, without emotional responsibilities to other people in the house, thinking this would keep me safe.

My relationship with my mother had not improved and she followed me out of the house every day, screaming at me not to return. I'd wait until the house was settled for the night and come back anyway because I didn't know what else to do or any place to go. One night she waited up for me and, as I opened the back door, she flew across the kitchen with her arm raised. My own arm moved instinctively in a defence motion and she backed off immediately.

'Don't you raise a hand to me, you little mongrel.'

I didn't tell her I had no intention of hitting her or that it was only a reflex defence action, because it worked in my favour. She never hit me again.

When she wasn't yelling at me to get out, she was telling me to get married. To whom it didn't matter. She still saw marriage as a way of getting rid of me for good. Not only would she be free of me, but I'd gain respectability as a married woman and she could hold her head up with pride. I'm not sure why it was she thought I had all these blokes just lining up to marry me, but she must have thought it was that easy.

The only person I wanted to marry was Michael and we wouldn't be able to do that for another year and, before the year was out, that plan was off as well. We both had too many unresolved issues to be able to make it work. We tried our hardest, but we got in the way of our own happiness. With our break up went the only constant in my life. For four years, through all the forced separations and unhappiness, I'd held on to the belief we'd eventually build a life together. The rose covered cottage, the six children, the perfect marriage was over before it had a chance to begin.

I was on my own.

'Why don't you get married and let someone else have the worry of you?'

I heard the words so often I began to judge all males as their potential as a husband. I wanted to be looked after, to be loved and cherished. I felt as if I'd lived a hundred lifetimes and I was tired.

I peered intently at the face before me. The features were distantly familiar, but it was a stranger who looked back at me, eyes empty and features blank in resignation. The hair, backcombed into an unnatural lacquered beehive, towered above arched eyebrows and pale cheeks. The corners of the mouth set with the inevitability of life. A shower of pink net flowed above and around the face, as if to contain it and preserve the fragility of it. I struggled to find recognition.

Marcia stood next to me, watching and waiting for a response, but I continued to stare in bewilderment. She took a bottle of Boag's from a brown paper bag and pushed it towards me.

'I thought you might need this.'

This broke the spell and I laughed at her disregard of the house rules, at the bottle of beer standing incongruous on the scarred dressing table top, and at the situation I'd placed myself in.

'You don't have to go through with it,' she plucked the threads of doubt from my mind.

'I have to now. It's too late to back out.'

'No, it's not. Just go down and tell Mum you're not doing it. You're only seventeen for Christ's sake.'

Visions of my mother's wrath played out in my mind. The lifetime of control, unchecked psychological and physical abuse blurred reality. Standing here in the attic, the scene of so much fear and heartache, I knew I couldn't spend another night in this place. Flashbacks to the alternatives barred any hope of escape. *Regent House, Mount St Canice, Winbirra* and *Winlaton* were all behind me now. Any future incarceration could only be in a psychiatric ward or a prison cell and I knew she had the power to orchestrate this.

'I'm just too scared.'

She flicked the top off the bottle and the contents came to life in a puff of froth.

'Ah, come on, Bub, have a drink,' She raised the bottle in salute, 'here's to us, mate.'

I stood in a froth of pink on the church steps, my new husband a stranger at my side, as we faced a small crowd of well-wishers. In the street below a familiar face looked up at me and I locked eyes with Michael for a brief instant, before he gunned the motor of his car and took off in a haze of smoked rubber. The dream was finally over and my new life had begun.

Elbow length gloves covered the tattoos on my forearm, and flesh coloured Band-Aids concealed my upper arms from the scrutiny of the wedding guests, while my new husband hid his consumption of alcohol in visits to the bathroom, and behind outbuildings and shrubs. Our wedding night was spent unconsummated, while he snored in an alcohol induced stupor and I pondered the terrible wrong I'd done to both of us. This beginning formed the foundation for my marriage, but I kept my feelings hidden and played the part of the new bride.

Epilogue

Through adoption, I became one of the stolen generations of white children, taken at birth and raised in a family so culturally and spiritually distant from my own genetic heritage I was left to flounder in a sea of disconnection. Unable to conform to the expectations of those vested with my care, I was removed from the home, through unsanctioned welfare intervention and placed in institutions of punishment.

I have worked hard throughout my life to overcome the stigma of these early experiences, to turn them into a positive base on which to build my life, family and career. I believe I succeeded in this until events beyond my control, by way of government enquiries etc. forced me to relive my past on almost a daily basis. I never expected, in my older age, to have no choice in the reliving of my failed adoption and subsequent institutional care, through the almost constant barrage over the past ten or more years of enquiry after enquiry, apology after apology, via the print, radio and television media, social media and through my email account. This is not something I have desired nor sought, but my needs and those of others like me, who chose to live our lives without the burden of the past, have been given no say in the matter.

Winlaton changed me forever. It affirmed the negative self-image impressed upon me since my birth and left me vulnerable to the control of others. Despite an exterior of assertiveness I've created over the years, I continue to take the line of least resistance when the potential for conflict arises and find this happens with greater frequency since the inquiries. The obligatory, but empty, apologies that followed have taken what little peace of mind I had, dragging me back to a time I've worked hard to forget.

So often these inquiries made subtle distinctions between institutions to separate the deserving from the undeserving as well as shifting the timelines to suit the agendas of the stake holders. This secondary abuse has set up class distinctions within the Forgotten

Australian communities, adding to feelings of alienation and perpetuating low self-esteem and sense of personal worth. Healing, whatever that may mean to each individual, has resulted for few, while there has been an increase in post-traumatic stress related conditions for many. Too many Forgotten Australians have gone from survivor to victim, as they seek the holy grail of compensation, needing to maintain the required level of trauma outcome if they are to be successful in their claim.

I'm neither proud nor ashamed to have been in Winlaton. My life has been what it has been. I cannot change the past I thought I'd said goodbye to half a century ago, but I wish I could change the here and now and not have it dangled in front of me as some sort of permanent reprimand and reminder of that which cannot be changed.

Victorian Government Apology

Apology from:
Premier Steven Bracks on behalf of the government of Victoria

9th August 2006

The Victorian apology was delivered in the Victorian parliament on 9 August 2006 by the then Premier Steve Bracks. The standing orders of the parliament were suspended to allow the Premier, the leaders of the Liberal and National parties and the Minister for Community Services to make statements. The apology was:

The government of Victoria welcomes the report of the Senate Community Affairs References Committee, Forgotten Australians, which was tabled in the Senate on 30 August 2004, as it offers an opportunity to offer a public statement of apology about some of the past practices in the provision of out-of-home care services in Victoria.

The report provides a detailed picture of the life experiences of many people who as children spent all or part of their childhood in institutional care across Australia. The experiences of many of these children were distressing and have had an enduring detrimental effect on their lives. The Victorian government believes it is important that these histories are known, are heard and are acknowledged.

The government is working hard to ensure that those unacceptable past practices are never ever again experienced by any Victorian child.

We acknowledge that there have been failures with respect to many children entrusted to care.

As a result of being placed in care, many of these children lost contact with their families.

The state, the churches and community agencies cared for thousands of children over the years. For those who were abused and neglected, the message we wish to give to them is that we acknowledge their pain and their hurt.

We are also committed to working together with survivors of abuse and neglect in care to promote the healing process.

We take the opportunity provided by the release of this report to express our deep regret and apologise sincerely to all of those who as children suffered abuse and neglect whilst in care and to those who did not receive the consistent loving care that every child needs and deserves.

The National Apology to people affected by forced adoption or removal policies and practices.

On 21 March 2013, the former Prime Minister Julia Gillard apologised on behalf of the Australian Government to people affected by forced adoption or removal policies and practices.
The national apology was delivered in the Great Hall of Parliament House, Canberra.National Apology for Forced Adoptions
21 March 2013

1. Today, this Parliament, on behalf of the Australian people, takes responsibility and apologises for the policies and practices that forced the separation of mothers from their babies, which created a lifelong legacy of pain and suffering.

2. We acknowledge the profound effects of these policies and practices on fathers.

3. And we recognise the hurt these actions caused to brothers and sisters, grandparents, partners and extended family members.

4. We deplore the shameful practices that denied you, the mothers, your fundamental rights and responsibilities to love and care for your children. You were not legally or socially acknowledged as their mothers. And you were yourselves deprived of care and support.

5. To you, the mothers who were betrayed by a system that gave you no choice and subjected you to manipulation, mistreatment and malpractice, we apologise.

6. We say sorry to you, the mothers who were denied knowledge of your rights, which meant you could not provide informed consent. You were given false assurances. You were forced to endure the coercion and brutality of practices that were unethical, dishonest and in many cases illegal.

7. We know you have suffered enduring effects from these practices forced upon you by others. For the loss, the grief, the disempowerment, the stigmatisation and the guilt, we say sorry.

8. To each of you who were adopted or removed, who were led to believe your mother had rejected you and who were denied the opportunity to grow up with your family and community of origin and to connect with your culture, we say sorry.

9. We apologise to the sons and daughters who grew up not knowing how much you were wanted and loved.

10. We acknowledge that many of you still experience a constant struggle with identity, uncertainty and loss, and feel a persistent tension between loyalty to one family and yearning for another.

11. To you, the fathers, who were excluded from the lives of your children and deprived of the dignity of recognition on your children's birth records, we say sorry. We acknowledge your loss and grief.

12. We recognise that the consequences of forced adoption practices continue to resonate through many, many lives. To you, the siblings, grandparents, partners and other family members who have shared in the pain and suffering of your loved ones or who were unable to share their lives, we say sorry.

13. Many are still grieving. Some families will be lost to one another forever. To those of you who face the difficulties of reconnecting with family and establishing ongoing relationships, we say sorry.

14. We offer this apology in the hope that it will assist your healing and in order to shine a light on a dark period of our nation's history.

15. To those who have fought for the truth to be heard, we hear you now. We acknowledge that many of you have suffered in silence for far too long.

16. We are saddened that many others are no longer here to share this moment. In particular, we remember those affected by these practices who took their own lives. Our profound sympathies go to their families.

17. To redress the shameful mistakes of the past, we are committed to ensuring that all those affected get the help they need, including access to specialist counselling services and support, the ability to find the truth in freely available records and assistance in reconnecting with lost family.

18. We resolve, as a nation, to do all in our power to make sure these practices are never repeated. In facing future challenges, we will remember the lessons of family separation. Our focus will be on protecting the fundamental rights of children and on the importance of the child's right to know and be cared for by his or her parents.

19. With profound sadness and remorse, we offer you all our unreserved apology.

Declaration of the Rights of the Child

All children have the right to what follows, no matter what their race, colour sex, language, religion, political or other opinion, or where they were born or who they were born to.

You have the special right to grow up and to develop physically and spiritually in a healthy and normal way, free and with dignity.

You have a right to a name and to be a member of a country.

You have a right to special care and protection and to good food, housing and medical services.

You have the right to special care if handicapped in any way.

You have the right to love and understanding, preferably from parents and family, but from the government where these cannot help.

You have the right to go to school for free, to play, and to have an equal chance to develop yourself and to learn to be responsible and useful.

Your parents have special responsibilities for your education and guidance.

You have the right always to be among the first to get help.

You have the right to be protected against cruel acts or exploitation, e.g. you shall not be obliged to do work which hinders your development both physically and mentally.

You should not work before a minimum age and never when that would hinder your health, and your moral and physical development. You should be taught peace, understanding, tolerance and friendship among all people.